# UNLOCKING OUR FENCED IN HEARTS

## By Listening to the Voice of Love

### Jan Wasco and Molly Keating

Workbook & Bible Study Included

PRESS

*Unlocking Our Fenced In Hearts*
*By Listening to the Voice of Love*
by Jan Wasco and Molly Keating

Printed in the United States of America

ISBN 978-1-60477-868-7

Unless otherwise indicated, Bible quotations are taken from The New American Bible (NAB), Copyright © 1990 by Oxford University Press, and The Holy Bible, The New International Version (NIV), Copyright © 1973, 1978, 1984 by International Bible Society, Zondervan Publishing House, and The New Jerusalem Bible (NJV), Copyright © 1999 by Doubleday, a division of Random House, Inc., and Darton, Longman & Todd Ltd., and The Holy Bible King James Version (KJV), Copyright © 2000 by Holman Bible Publishers, and The Amplified Bible Old Testament, Copyright © 1962, 1964 by Zondervan Publishing House, and The New King James Version (NKJV), Copyright © 1979, 1980, 1982 by Thomas Nelson Inc., Publishers, and The Holy Bible, New Century Version (NCV), Copyright © 1987, 1988, 1991 by Word Publishing, Dallas, Texas.

www.xulonpress.com

# Reviews

God created each of us with core needs which only God can meet. We are God-wired for unconditional love, security, and reinforcement of our personal worth. We want to know we are valued, unique and special. *Unlocking Our Fenced in Hearts* leads us on a path of self-discovery to determine the ways in which we have tried on our own to meet our core needs through means other than God. Jan and Molly share their stories with vulnerability and give us the wherewithal to find healing for the wounds we have incurred doing life without Christ. I highly recommend this book for those ready to bring their dysfunctional behaviors into the light and be made whole.

Reverend Dr. Roberta W. Cabot
Pastor of Wolf Lake United Methodist Church

I've just read *Unlocking Our Fenced in Hearts* and can hardly wait to share it with the women in my life. Jan and Molly have gotten to the very heart of our lives – we do build fences and our life experiences are unique as women. Sharing our stories may help to change the experience, not only in our own lives, but for the generations of women to follow.

Fences of Anger and Fences of Fear helped me to reignite my personal journey. I can see how many times I've let anger rule and fear control me. The combination of stories, research, scripture and probing questions leads to a deeper level of study than many similar tools that I've seen. Feeling God's presence, as I read the wisdom of women, shed new light on my own path.

Joyce Hagen-Flint
Past President, American Society of Healthcare Food
Service Administrators (ASHFSA)
Moderator, Board of Deacons, Grace Presbyterian Church,
Spring Hill, Florida

# Table of Contents

*"And He said, Go out and stand on the mountain before the Lord. And behold, the Lord passed by, and a great and strong wind rent the mountains and broke in pieces the rocks before the Lord, but the Lord was not in the wind; and after the wind an earthquake, but the Lord was not in the earthquake; and after the earthquake a fire, but the Lord was not in the fire; and after the fire (a sound of gentle stillness and) a still, small, voice."*
*1 Kings 19: 11-12 (The Amplified Bible: Old Testament)*

# Dedications

I thank God first and foremost in my life for his awesome love and his many blessings. I am especially thankful for my family whom I love with my whole heart. To my husband Ken who never stops encouraging me to be the person God created me to be. I love you Ken and thank you for sharing your life with me. I especially thank our daughters, Shannon, our editor, whose devoted patience and writing skills enabled us to write our thoughts using fewer words, and Lauren whose prayerful and calming influence has sustained me throughout this writing project. You three are my greatest gifts from God and I am a better person to have been loved by you.

I also thank my mother and father, Richard and Betty Larsen for raising me and being the first to introduce me to my Heavenly Father. I also want to thank my Theology professors, Sister Amata Fabbro, Dr. Robert Marko, and Sister Yvonne Greiner, who have mentored me spiritually and have increased my love and study of the Scriptures and have helped me to grow in my faith. And finally, to my co-author and wonderful friend, and sister in Christ, Molly, and her supportive, loving, and encouraging husband Paul who helped format our manuscript.

*~Jan*

I would like to dedicate this book to the abiding Presence of Christ who dwells within each of us and to my husband Paul and my family. Thank you for your unfailing support and encouragement. I love you...

~Molly

# Acknowledgements

S hannon L. Wasco— Our love and appreciation for your dedicated approach to the editing of this manuscript; the result of which more concisely conveys our passionate thoughts and ideas.

God has blessed you with a great love for the written word.

Paul Flinsky— Thank you for your skillful formatting of this text and your grace filled patience with fledgling authors. You are a true professional at your craft.

Ken, Shannon, Lauren, and Mai— We could never have done this without your love, support and prayers. I love you all!

Sister Amata Fabbro— For all of your mentoring, and spiritual insights and for helping me to fall even more deeply in love with the Scriptures.

Dr. Robert Marko— For challenging me to dig deeper into my faith and to believe in myself.

Sister Yvonne Greiner—For teaching me the many ways of prayer.

To Jeff Fitzgerald and the helpful Staff at Xulon Press— God bless you for your perseverance and encouragement in getting us to get our manuscript in.

Molly— I could never have done this without my dear spiritual friend by my side. I love you!

Jan— When God gifted me with your friendship, my heart lightened, my passion intensified, and we became a beautiful instrument of God's love. Thank you. I love you!

To you the Reader—May you free your hearts, find your God Voice and start living a life of love.

And to our Awesome God— May our love for you and the joy in which we wrote this book bring you glory, honor and praise.

# Prologue

*"Ask and it will be given to you; seek and you will find; knock and the door will be opened to you. For everyone who asks, receives; and the one who seeks, finds; and to the one who knocks, the door will be opened." (Matthew 7:7, 8)(NAB)*

We invite you to unlock and open the gate to the fence that you have built around your life and your relationships; to step into a world where there are no walls and no barriers. A world where all of us can rediscover our "inner divine voice" by dismantling the fences that keeps our words invisible.

The late Henri Nouwen, one of the most influential contemporary authors on Christian spirituality, wrote about the importance of listening to the inner voice of the heart. Nouwen speaks of the necessity, "to be empty, free, and open, conscious of God-with-us, sensing God present, listening with our hearts to the voice of love." This voice that Nouwen refers to can be none other than our God voice. The beckoning of the Holy Spirit, the *still small voice* of a loving God, invites us to experience God's grace and loving presence by tearing down the fences around our hearts.

It is Christ's love that tears down the fence, and it is our faith that builds the bridge. God's grace alone has the power to change us. When our hearts come to know God's grace it is then that our lives are renewed and we are forever transformed. In the movie, *"The Passion of the Christ,"* we were particularly moved by one line that Jesus uttered. "My heart is ready, Father!" It was as if Christ's heart had been on a journey and was now so full of love that he was ready to die for us. When we strip away all the outside noise and listen to that often dormant little whisper, it transforms our journey. When we feel centered and enveloped in a sense of peace we can reverberate in a joyful "Yes!" to the call of the Spirit. This is salvation; that wondrous pilgrimage that starts from within and works to tear down all the fences we have erected around our heart. This is where God finds us. St. Augustine's prayer, "Our hearts are restless until we find our rest in Thee," resonates inside each one of us. This freedom to choose is truly a wondrous gift. It is a personal choice that is prompted from an interior movement. This is the most excellent path we can choose for ourselves; to allow the power of God's love to transform us into the incredible person that God has created each of us to be. Let the journey begin!

In each of the seven chapters the reader will find special icons that are designed to call particular attention to the workbook section of the text. In these sections the reader can interact with the text through scripture study, reflection, journaling, and sharing of their own personal experiences and stories.

**Taking it to Heart**

**Scripture Reflections**

**Prayer Affirmations**

**Work book Questions**

**Journaling from the Heart**

# Introduction

*"Love is the master key that opens the gates of happiness."*
Oliver Wendell Holmes

Walls and fences are everywhere and no age or race can escape being effected in some way by their pernicious power. These menacing forces have impacted our lives for generations. These self-imposed barriers fragment and isolate us from God's love and from each other. They are what keep people apart and make them distrustful and suspicious of one another. Our personal fences have the power to destroy fellowship and our intimate relationships as they breed prejudice and deteriorate our self esteem. The following story by Anthony De Mello, one of the great spiritual masters of our time illustrates this universal inner struggle.

Once at a country fair, there was a little black boy who was fascinated by the man selling balloons. He watched as the balloon man deliberately cut loose and released a bright red balloon that soared high into the sky above, attracting a crowd of prospective customers. Next, he watched carefully as the balloon man released a blue balloon, then a yellow one, and finally a white one, each soaring high up into the sky until they no longer could be seen. The little black boy stood next to the balloon man for a long time, and then asked, *"Sir, if you sent the black one up, would it go as high as the others?"* The balloon man gave the boy an understanding smile. He snipped the string that held the black balloon in place and, as it soared upwards he said, *"It isn't the color, son. It's what's inside that makes it rise."*

The balloon man in the story represents the love of God that tears down the fences/walls of prejudice that divide us. The fences that say to us that one person is better than another. We sense while reading this story that the young boy wonders whether his black colored balloon can rise as high as the others. He has already in his short time on earth questioned whether that black balloon in some way represents himself, and questions if it is as good as the other colored balloons.

At some point in that little boy's life he began to see the differences between himself and others based on the color of his skin, it was then that the fence of low self-esteem was born. These self doubts grew and made the boy question his own distinctiveness. It is the balloon man's insightful words that deliver the important message we all need to hear, *"It isn't the color son that makes the balloon rise it's what's inside."* It is not what man's fences of prejudice and low self-esteem have dictated to him about self worth rather it is the qualities we possess inside. We are all equal in God's eyes, what really makes us different is what's inside our hearts and what we choose to do with the gifts God gave us.

*"What lies behind us and what lies before us are tiny matters, compared to what lies within us"* Ralph Waldo Emerson

# 1

# FENCES BUILT BY SELF DOUBTING

### Embrace your Identity in Christ

As human beings, we build up a lifetime of walls and fences, which are built on a foundation of self doubt, fear of failure, and of never thinking we are good enough. Much of our identity is wrapped up in what we imagine others think about us, instead of relying on what God alone loves about us. Our sense of value, worth, and success should come from God and not from the world. When we embrace our identity in Christ we can be transformed into the person that God created us to be. When we have Christ dwelling within our hearts, extraordinary things can happen. Through Christ living in our unique personalities and in the ordinary circumstances of our lives, we are transformed. God does not call any of us to be perfect, but he does call us to be secure in his love and aware of his indwelling presence.

### Striving for Perfection

*Molly* ~ Scripture tells us that *"You must be perfect just as your heavenly Father is perfect" (Mt 5:48).* Many of us cannot realize our potential for a deep spiritual life because perfection is such an unattainable goal. This desire to reach the unreachable is something I know from experience.

I believe my need to be perfect surfaced in the 8th grade. I had been a good student up until then, but one report card marking I brought home all A's and one "C" in history. I can still hear my Dad asking, *"What's with the 'C'?"* Looking back, I am sure he meant it as an off-hand remark, but something changed inside me that day. I suddenly felt not good enough. I began high school with a deep-seated feeling and desire to be perfect. My first marking period at Bishop Foley I received straight A's, a perfect 4.0. Not one to rest on my laurels, I felt compelled to repeat that, each semester, for the next four years. I graduated Valedictorian with a G.P.A. of 4.2 due to honors classes. However, I have found through a life time of experiences that maintaining that level of perfection is difficult because often one loses sight of what they may be giving up in striving to achieve it. I believe I lost part of my soul in my obsession over grades. The perfect grades became the almighty idol and I desired to achieve what each teacher seemed to demand I earn - that first letter of the alphabet.

I recall now how unavailable I became to friends and family when exam time rolled around. I was possessed by the need to excel. The irony was that I wasn't a gifted student, and school did not come easily. I was just driven to study and apply myself to the extreme so my accomplishment would validate me. In a world where love often felt conditional, school was my arena for self-esteem. Success was my prayer. God for me was far away. He was distant, omnipotent, and another someone to please. Like one of my teachers, I wanted an "A" in his classroom and needed to know what was expected of me so I could invoke his favor and approval.

After graduating from high school I headed off to the University of Michigan on a nursing scholarship. High school had been a challenge but nothing could have prepared me for the culture shock of Ann Arbor. I grew up with "Doby Gillis," and I thought college would be about sororities, capezios and meeting at the malt shop. U of M at the time was about Vietnam protests, drug use, bra-burning and the Students for a Democratic Society. It was wild and uncivilized. Everyone was a Valedictorian, so academia was not an area where I could easily excel. Subconsciously, I chose control over something more destructive, or what I thought seemed that way; I became anorexic. My body became my palette for perfection. I was at a healthy weight going in to school but my anorexia changed that, by the time my Dad came to take me home two years later I weighed only 72 pounds and I never went back. I felt like the ultimate failure, something I had never felt until that moment. My parents took me to a counselor, who helped me realize the insidious aspect of the disease is that often the patient does not want to get better. Gaining weight becomes a symbol of losing control and that fear consumed me at the same time I was literally starving to death. Through therapy my obsession with food continued, it was my constant focus and after everything I had lost and the people I had hurt I started to turn to it for consolation and comfort. I began to eat back everything I had once considered forbidden. The emotional void within me was so large that massive amounts of food would not fill it. All the sugary, starchy foods were comforting, they became my friends. They made me feel better. They provided immediate self-gratification and during the ingestion and the calm that followed, I felt numb to the pain of the outside world and my suffering within.

I recall driving around one Halloween night soon after, watching the kids running around the neighborhood trick or treating. They looked so carefree and innocent; I began to wonder why inside I felt neither. I remember thinking I did not want to live anymore. In the midst of all these people

21

celebrating I had never felt more lonely. I cried out to God: *"Help me Lord; I can not do this anymore, it is just you and me."* That night while sitting alone in my car begging him to come into my heart, a most wonderful thing happened - the deep sense of despair seemed to lift off my shoulders. I knew it would not be easy, but from that moment on, I felt I would never be alone again. It was a liberating experience, but it was only the beginning of the ongoing process which was occurring on an interior level. It initiated a profound desire in my heart to respond and to listen to God's will for my life. It was definitely a turning point in my road to recovery. I realized there were no heroes that were going to rescue me. It seemed so overwhelming at the time, but my new found personal relationship with God gave me the inner strength to want to succeed again but this time with the Spirit's guidance, comfort and consolation.

Ron DelBene, in his book, *The Hunger of the Heart: A Call to Spiritual Growth,* helped me to understand this need for perfection by elaborating on the word "perfection" itself. In the original Greek, perfection means whole, integrated, or together, and for many people this interpretation opens an entirely new way of looking at their spiritual potential. Personally, in this way I saw the balance of what that integration should look like. The physical, mental, emotional, and spiritual dynamic of who I was encompassed the whole of me; my strengths and my weaknesses. God loves me just the way I am. God accepts me right where I am. The mistakes, poor choices, and suffering are all things I can share with him and through discernment he humanizes me to others.

Trying to maintain perfection only alienated me from realizing my full potential. The spiritual journey is a spiraling course of growth. It is not a ladder mentality where we keep stepping closer to God. God is within our hearts. The closer we draw to God, the closer we draw to each other and the more authentic we become.

All of us at some point in our lives must have experienced times where we questioned who we really are and what our life is really all about. We get caught up in what we think others and the world wants from us. Thus we forget about what God really created us to be. As Christians we desire to live authentically in the truth of who we are in Christ, and yet at the same time we are afraid of any suffering that this might cause us. Criticism, persecution, rejection, abandonment, and not being loved or accepted for who we are, are among our greatest fears. These fears can cause low self-esteem which prompts us to build fences around ourselves to keep out any suffering. Sadly, some prefer to live behind those self-erected fences for protection, rather then hoping and looking for the possibility to break through the barriers and experience an encounter with the Divine.

### Right Choices rise above Perfection

*Jan* ~ I am reminded of the fence I erected called low self-esteem when I think back on the time in my life when I thought that grades were more important than choices. Already holding a bachelors degree from Michigan State University I had decided that I wanted to fully and completely understand the discipline of Theology. I knew that I needed to start at its beginnings and so I decided to return to the classroom. I found myself quickly on the road to earning another bachelors degree, this time at Aquinas College in the discipline of Theology. Returning to college in my forties took a great deal of prayer, discernment, and courage. Yet I knew that I had a strong desire to study something I felt passionate about and I had always longed to study about God and his teachings.

Earning a second bachelor degree allows one to transfer certain credits from your first Bachelors. After completing my Theology classes at Aquinas and earning a 3.98 GPA, I was dismayed to hear that classes that I had taken over twenty five years ago would also be calculated in determining whether I qualified for their academic award. Therefore, when I graduated I was not allowed to wear the academic cords. This fact caused me great embarrassment; especially in knowing that my professors would see me during the graduation ceremony without gold cords adorning my graduation gown.

My self-esteem had taken a beating and I remember how hurt and depressed I felt just prior to graduation day. One particular evening, as I broke down in front of my daughter, I will never forget her wise and spiritual response to my depression. She said, I was responding to God calling me. She let me know just how proud she was of me listening to God's voice and then choosing to be obedient to it. That night, she reminded me of why I chose to study Theology in the first place. It was not about the recognition or the gold cords rather it had to do with growing closer to God and bringing Christ to others. She really made me aware of what was most important when she shared a quote from one of her favorite books, *Harry Potter and the Chamber of Secrets*, by *J.K. Rowling,* In the movie version, Professor Dumbledore tells young Harry Potter, *"It is not our abilities that shows us what we truly are it is our choices."* She then looked deeply into my eyes as if they were a window into my soul and said, *"Mom, you followed your heart and chose to listen to God and that says more about whom you truly are then any grade, diploma or gold cord."*

Too often, we let a fence of this world, such as self doubt and low self-esteem prevent us from answering the call of the Divine. Our desire should be to search within our hearts for our God voice and then to have the courage to use it in order to become the person that God created us to be despite the cost. The following reflection signifies a time in all of our lives where our fears can hold us back from being who we really are.

**Reflection:** <u>*The Mask that hides*</u> *Author unknown*
*Don't be fooled by me. Don't be fooled by the face I wear.*
*I wear a thousand masks that I'm afraid to take off- and*
*none of them are me!*

*I give the impression that I'm secure: that all is sunny*
*and unruffled within, as well as without; that confidence is*
*my name and coolness my game; that the water is calm and*
*I need no one. But don't believe me...please!*

*My surface may seem smooth, but my surface is a mask.*
*Beneath dwells the real me in confusion, in fear, in alone-*
*ness. But, I hide this. I panic at the thought of my weakness*
*and frantically created a mask to hide behind, to shield me*
*from the glance that knows.*

*Yet, such a glance is precisely my salvation-I know it. If*
*it is followed by acceptance and by love. It is the only thing*
*that will assure me of what I cannot assure myself that I am*
*worth something.*

*But I do not tell you this. I don't dare. I'm afraid to. So,*
*I play my game, my desperate game, with a façade of assur-*
*ance without, and a trembling child within. So begins the*
*parade of masks. And my, life becomes a front.*

*I idly chatter to you...surface and top-of-the-head talk,*
*saying nothing of what is crying within me. Please listen*
*carefully and try to hear what I am NOT saying-what I would*
*like to be able to say- what for survival I need to say-but*
*what I cannot say.*

*I dislike hiding...honestly! I'd really like to be genuine*
*and spontaneous, and ME-but you've got to help me. You've*

*got to hold out your hand, even when that is the last thing I seem to want.*

*Each time you are kind, and gentle, and encouraging... each time you try to understand me because you care, my heart grows wings-very small wings, very feeble wings, but wings. With your sensitivity and sympathy, and your power of understanding, you can breathe life into me. I want you to know that.*

*You can help me to be the creator of the person that is me, if you choose to. You can break down the wall and release me from behind my mask... my shadow world of panic and uncertainty...from my lonely self. Don't pass me by. I may fight against the very help I need. But try to beat down those walls with gentle hands of love and sympathy...firm but gentle hands... for a child is sensitive.*

*Who I am, you may wonder. I may be every man and woman you will meet.*

**Taking it to Heart**

Our true identity and what gives meaning and purpose to our lives comes from our relationship with God, and with others. Next time you ask who am I, it might be better to ask yourself who are you in Christ? Or more importantly, how can you contribute to the building up of the Body of Christ? The following reflection echoes the importance of what makes life meaningful.

## REFLECTION:

### A Creed for Life (*Author unknown*)

*Don't undermine your worth by comparing yourself to others.*
*It is because we are different that each of us is special.*

*Don't set your goals by what other people deem important.*
*Only God knows what is best for you.*

*Don't take for granted the things closest to your heart.*
*Cling to them as you would your life,*
*for without them, life is meaningless.*

*Don't let life slip through your fingers,*
*by living in the past or only for the future.*
*Living your life one day at a time,*
*you live all the days of your life.*
*Don't give up when you still have something to give.*
*Nothing is really over until the moment you stop trying.*

*Don't be afraid to admit that you are less than perfect.*
*It is this fragile thread that binds us to each other.*

*Don't be afraid to encounter risks.*
*It is by taking chances that we learn to be brave.*

*Don't shut love out of your life.*
*By saying it is impossible to find.*

*The quickest way to receive love*
*is to give it wings.*

*Don't dismiss your dreams*
*to be without dreams is to be without hope.*
*To be without hope, is to be without purpose.*

*Don't run through life so fast that you forget*
*not only where you've been,*
*but also where you are going.*

*Life is not just a race,*
*but a disciplined journey*
*to be Savored each step of the way.*

## Living through Christ

Life is a journey, a passage that holds many obstacles along the way. We all need God as our compass so that we can be better equipped to maneuver up and over those false walls/fences. Fences that hold us back from experiencing a life truly lived by and through the Spirit of God. Each of us has been given special gifts and talents that make us unique and different- not better than each other. When we decide to use those gifts to make the world a better place then and only then have we succeeded in using them for God's purpose. The question that we must answer is- who am I allowing to penetrate my spirit and make me feel as though I am not good enough? Eleanor Roosevelt once said, "No one can make you feel inferior without your consent." Why then do I give so much power to others to decide whether or not I fit in? Why do I gauge my self esteem by what others think of me instead of rejoicing in the reasons God created and loves me? If you were asked to write your own "Creed for Life" what would it say?

## My Creed For Life

_____
_____
_____
_____
_____
_____
_____
_____
_____
_____
_____
_____
_____
_____
_____
_____
_____
_____
_____
_____
_____
_____
_____
_____
_____

**Scripture Reflections:**

**Romans 8:26** *"The Spirit too comes to the aid of our weakness; for we do not know how to pray as we ought, but the Spirit itself intercedes with Inexpressible groaning."* *(NAB)*

**1 Corinthians 2:9** *"What not eye has seen, nor ear heard, not the human heart conceived, what God has prepared for those who love Him."* *(NRSV)*

**1 Corinthians 3:16** *"Do you not know that you are temple of God and that the Spirit of God dwells in you?"(NAB)*

**Hosea 2:16** *"So I am going to lure her; I will lead her into the desert and speak to her heart."* *(NAB)*

**2 Corinthians 5:17** *"If any man is in Christ, he is a new creature"*

**Colossians 1:22** *"Regardless of how imperfect we think we are "He {Jesus} has now reconciled you in His fleshy body through death, in order to present you before Him holy and blameless and beyond reproach."(NIV)*

**Romans 12:2** *"Therefore, reprogram your thoughts as St. Paul said and, "Be transformed by the renewing of your mind."* *(NIV)*

Look up **John 16:27** and **Isaiah 43:1-5** what do these passages have in common? How does God free us to love ourselves and others?

**John 16:27** _____

_____

_____

_____

_____

_____

**Isaiah 43:1, 5** _____

_____

_____

_____

_____

**Psalm 139:13-14** captures our worth as seen from God's eyes. After reading the Psalm reflect on what each phrase means to you. Write a short description of your reflection below.

_____

_____

_____

_____

_____

Walk in what the Bible calls the *"newness of life"* *(Romans 6:4)*. Leave your old identity behind and change the patterns that you have developed of low self worth in your past. Interact with the world and your environment as the person God has intended you to be. I am reminded of an old Christian Hymn when I think of this new relationship that I have with Christ. It was written by C. Austin Miles (1868-1941), it is entitled: In the Garden.

*In the Garden*
  *I come to the garden alone,*
  *while the dew is still on the roses;*
  *and the voice I hear, falling on my ear,*
  *the Son of God discloses.*
  *And He walks with me and he talks with me,*
  *and he tells me I am His own.*
  *And the joys we share as we tarry there,*
  *none other has ever known.*

**Workbook Questions**

1. What fences/masks do you hide behind?

2. What gives your life meaning and purpose?

3. How does a good relationship with God help your self esteem?

4. How do you find and listen to your God voice?

5. What negative patterns do you see repeating themselves in your own life that keeps you from being the person God created you to be?

6. What fences of low self esteem do you erect?

7. In what ways might you reach out and love those who are hurting?

8. Who in your life do you allow to hold the keys to your identity?

9. What we think about ourselves becomes our perspective as how we see ourselves.
   Which of these statements sound like you?

   A. *I must have a sign on my forehead that says "Take advantage of me."*
   B. *Everyone is always so helpful and accommodating?*

10. Each of the above beliefs will create quite different experiences. Usually what we believe about ourselves becomes our experience. We also tend to treat ourselves the way our parents treated us. What did you hear most often as a child?

    A. *You never seem to do anything right. If only you'd...*
    B. *You are an awesome person. I love you.*

11. How often do you punish yourself or feel guilty?

12. How often do you tell yourself that you are doing a terrific job...that you are a lovely person?

13. We frequently add that we don't do enough, or that we don't deserve to be happy. Does that sound like you? What do you think is the difference between being happy and having found joy in your life? And why is joy more lasting?

14. Are you implicitly implying that you're not good enough? Whose standards are you judging yourself against? Whom do you need to please? Why? If this is your self-concept than how can you have possibly created the life that you now enjoy?

15. Can we change our attitudes about the past? Do you want to? Why or why not?

16. Can we see our life from another's perspective?

17. What do you think it was like for your parents when they were raising you and your siblings?

18. Can you forgive them for the mistakes they made?

19. As you become older, do you find yourself becoming more tolerant and forgiving, or more judgmental and bitter?

20. How does God want you to feel about yourself and others?

**Prayer Affirmations:**

1. Releasing the past, I accept the opportunity to begin anew today.

2. I am a beautiful child of God, thanks be to Jesus.

3. I rejoice in me. I am a wondrous expression of life and God's design.

4. Intelligence, strength, and self-esteem are always present. It is great to be alive.

5. I recognize my self-worth. I am good enough.

6. I know now that I am worthwhile. It is okay for me to succeed.

7. At every age, I love and respect myself.

8. Do you need me? I am there.

9. I feel safe to be me.

10. I give myself permission to be all that I can be and I love and appreciate myself and others.

11. Knowing that God loves me frees me to love myself and others.

12. I am a wondrous child of God made in God's own image and likeness.

**Journaling from the Heart**

Give an example of a story in your life that reflects an experience of how low self-esteem became a fence or barrier that impeded you from being the person God created you to be.

_____

_____

_____

_____

_____

_____

_____

_____

_____

_____

_____

_____

_____

_____

_____

_____

_____

_____

_____

_____

_____

_____

# 2

# FENCES THAT KEEP OTHERS OUT

## Learning to Live in Community

*"When your heart responds instinctively to other people's joys and sorrow, you will know you have lost your self and attained the experience of your "one-body-ness" with the human race- and love has finally arrived."*

Anthony De Mello

What is it that actually makes each of us unique? If we truly are brothers and sisters in Christ why do we so often fail to see each other in that light? Why do we compose rules and enforce laws that divide us from what God calls us to be, one Body of Christ?

Rita Snowden, a Methodist Minister, tells a story where church ceremonial law built a fence to keep others out. The story comes from the Second World War, the setting is France. It is a tale of a few unnamed soldiers, along with their sergeant, who brought home the body of their dead comrade to have him buried. The priest told them gently that he was bound to ask if their comrade had been a baptized member of the Roman Catholic Church. The men sadly did not know and thus the priest could not permit burial in his churchyard. The soldiers then sullenly took their comrade and buried him just outside the fence of the cemetery. The very next day the soldiers came back to visit the grave of their friend and to their astonishment they could not find it. As they were about to leave in anger and bewilderment, the priest came and told them that his heart had been troubled because of his refusal to allow the dead soldier to be buried in the churchyard. Early that morning, he had risen from his bed and with his own hands had moved the fence to include the body of the soldier who had died for his country.

It is amazing what love can do. The rules and regulations of a religion put up the fence, but it was the love of God within the priest that moved it. Jesus established a religion based on love and not rules. Jesus removes the fences around our hearts so that we are able to love others as he loves us.

### Rules made by Man

*Jan~* When I think of church made rules I am reminded of yet another story. This story is my own and takes place almost 60 years ago. My mother was Catholic and my father Protestant. It was my mother's dream to be married in her family church. Unfortunately, at that time the Catholic Church refused to marry them on account of my father being Protestant. My mother, with hard pressed determination began asking other Catholic parish priests if they could be wed in their church. After countless attempts, one priest finally agreed to allow them to be married, but on one condition. They were not allowed to walk down the center aisle of the church. My father's love for my mother showed its strength and commitment in his decision to go along with the priest's conditions. My mother's love for her Catholic faith was strong enough not to turn away from it, even when rules got in the way. I am grateful that neither of them chose to build a fence around their hearts.

I often wonder what God must have thought on that sacramental day, when religion or the priest's interpretation of certain rules decided to build a fence. Two devout Christians from two different faith practicing traditions, found the strength in their love. They listened to the voice of God in their hearts and found a way to be married in church. Unfortunately, they had to sacrifice a part of who they were in Christ when church rules prevented them from reciting their vows at the main altar.

*Molly*~ I recall a story from the spring of 1968. It was in my final year at St. Dennis grade school. A special Mass had been planned for our class. At the time, I was infatuated with a boy named Dan. When we were both asked to do the readings for the liturgy, I was more excited to be reading with Dan, than having the honor to read God's Word at Mass. One afternoon, while practicing for the event, Sr. Mary John called for the readers. We both went up towards the altar and there she calmly explained that Dan would stand at the podium where the priest read from, and I would read from a microphone set up next to the organ. My microphone was on the other side of the communion rail and approximately fifty feet from the altar. As I took my place far away, I was made aware that Dan and I were not seen as equals simply because of my gender. The communion rail symbolized a fence-like barrier that profoundly touched me as a young girl. And as I look back I realize that the experience that was high lighted by an innocent crush was really a metaphor for the "crush" or oppression of many women's voices in a Church that often reflects a patriarchal hierarchy. Today women's roles are wide and varied. We are being valued for our gifts to a myriad of ministries. But there are always new boundaries to recognize, fresh walls to deconstruct. How do we make peace with that? As women, we have serious issues to overcome.

We are restricted. Christian teaching and practice have often supported these restrictions and God-images that we have grown up with are often laden with negative effects. The crisis of credibility regarding authority is evident. I believe however, that with the power of the Holy Spirit directing us, we will find our way.

There is a dawning awareness of the interconnectedness between oppression of women and the domination of the poor and the earth itself. That is why I have found it so important to find a compassionate small faith community that affirms women and where I feel comfortable to speak my voice. We need to be who we are. And that is female Christians ministering in the Body of Christ. How can we do that? To me knowledge is power. The more I can learn about the great spiritual thinkers and teachers such as Catherine of Siena, Hildegard, Theresa of Avila, etc. the more I can draw closer to my authentic self by reflecting, sharing, and praying. For me centering prayer and quieting myself so I can hear the divine in the stillness affirms or nudges me to go deeper.

Wilkie Au's book, <u>By Way of the Heart</u>, gave me some wonderful insights on where I am on my own spiritual journey. As with any trip, we reach the destination only gradually. The irony of my spiritual passage is that I will not reach my destination of union with God while I am still alive. If I am going to stay on the road, however irregular it is, I must take courage in God's abiding presence along the way. My expectations of a flawless journey are counter-productive because it misrepresents the process of developmental growth. I need to find my voice in a Church that has often felt remote and detached and then I need to welcome all to the Banquet. The Church too is on a journey and when I begin to feel centered and calm enough to be present to the Spirit, I hope I can be a part of a community of inclusivity and diversity. A part of a holy place, where all are treated with dignity and respect, and the Body of Christ, like the human body will be in perfect harmony and balance.

In the language of poetry, Rainier Maria Rilke in her book <u>Rilke's Book of Hours</u> says this:

*God speaks to each of us as God makes us*
*And walks with us silently out of the night*
*These are the words we dimly hear:*
*You, sent out beyond your recall,*
*Go to the limits of your longing.*
*Embody me.*
*Flare up like flame*
*And make big shadows I can move in.*
*Let everything happen to you; beauty and terror.*
*Just keep going. No feeling is final.*
*Don't let yourself lose me.*
*Nearby is the country they call life.*
*You will know it by it seriousness*
Give me your hand.

This is my prayer for the Church, ministry, and for myself...

## God Sees our Hearts

*Jan~* What is it that really keeps us from loving others as Christ loves us? Why do we build up walls and put up fences to keep others out? The more I thought about it the more I realized that perhaps we have failed at being aware of who God created us to be, and who others are in Christ. Somewhere within this uncharted state of consciousness, we fail to really see others as God sees them. Our God voice becomes clouded by the world which fills our minds with an endless chatter of prejudice and man-made rules. What we think we know about other people takes over instead of focusing on what God sees when God looks into their hearts.

Can you recall a time when you misunderstood or misperceived another person's intentions, actions or character? Have we not all been guilty of jumping to conclusions, putting our foot in our mouth, or spreading unsubstantiated gossip about another human being? Why do I do that? Why do any of us do that? Again, could it be our lack of awareness of not being in touch with our God voice? God sends his very Spirit to live deep within all of our hearts. May the eyes of our hearts be enlightened.

## Aware of God's Presence

Being aware is realizing that God has always been there; God is everywhere and is in all. There is an old tale about a poor little fish who spent his days swimming in the ocean asking everyone, *"Excuse me, I am looking for the ocean can you please tell me where I might be able to find it?"* As humans, we search for God throughout our lives, often failing to realize that he is always with us. God reveals his presence to us everyday but we must open our eyes and our hearts to him. Jesus promised his Disciples that he would ask the Father to send them another Counselor to be with them forever, and as he ascended, he also said, *"Lo, I am with you always"* (Matthew 28:20 RSV).

*Jan* ~ I can recall one summer afternoon when my neighbor was frantically searching for her lost 2 year old son. I immediately helped her scour the neighborhood. During the search some of my worst fears surfaced. I thought about the lake nearby and the creek that ran behind her house. After hours of helping her she found him safely sleeping only a few feet from where her search originally began. In her frantic worry to find her son she missed seeing him If only we would learn to just look and see with our hearts, (the very center of our God voice) then and only then can we be truly present to God and fully understand that God is always there right beside us.

Cardinal Martini, the Archbishop of Milan, shares a story about a young Italian couple who were making plans for their upcoming marriage. Their parish priest had agreed to marry them and because they did not have a lot of money he also agreed to allow them to hold their reception in the parish courtyard. Unfortunately, the day of their wedding it poured rain and they were no longer able to have their reception outside so they begged the priest,

*"Would it be all right if we had the celebration in the church?"* Father was not too happy about holding a reception inside of church and his nonverbal behavior reflected his disapproval, but they pleaded further, *"We will eat a little cake, sing a little song, drink a little wine, and then go home."* Father hesitantly agreed to their request. As the night progressed the boisterous Italians that they were drank a little wine, sang a little song, then drank a little more wine, and sang a few more songs and within a short time their quiet little reception had turned into a great celebration. Everyone was enjoying themselves and having a grand time except Father who was nervously pacing up and down in the sacristy. He was overwrought by all of the noise that was coming from the wedding celebration in the church. Seeing the nervousness of the priest, the associate pastor tried to calm him down by asking, *"Father, is everything alright?"* Anxiously, the priest responded. *"Of course, I am not alright!' just listen to all of the noise that they are making in the House of God for heaven's sake!"*

"Well, Father, they really had no other place to go."

*"I know that! But do they have to make all that racket?"*

*"Well, we mustn't forget that Jesus himself was once present at a wedding!"* A moment passed before Father spoke quite frankly saying, *"I know Jesus Christ was present at a wedding banquet! But they didn't have the Blessed Sacrament there!!*

The priest failed to see beyond the rules established by man. I believe the associate pastor was trying to remind his colleague that Christ lives within each of us; he surrounds us with his love. He is not only made accessible through certain means, but his presence can even be felt in the most menial of all work that we do. Brother Lawrence, the great seventeenth-century saint and mystic, spent much of his life in the monastery kitchen among the dirty dishes, and he would say: *"I felt Jesus Christ as close to me in the kitchen as ever I did at the Blessed Sacrament."* The sacrament of marriage is about two people uniting in Christ. It is a sacramental celebration of God's love but when we are too hung up on church as an institution we often forget that Jesus Christ is the incarnation of the living God in the flesh, and that Jesus sent his Holy Spirit to dwell within each of us. When we start making the practice of worship and the following of strict rules more important than the simple act of loving God and inviting him into our lives something is seriously wrong. For God is the quintessence of love. And through him alone our lives, like our marriages are then blessed.

## Called to be like Christ

Jesus Christ said clearly, *"not everyone who says to me, 'Lord, Lord,' will enter the kingdom of heaven, but he who does the will of My Father who is in heaven will enter. Matthew 7:21 (NAB)* God the Father, according to Christ is more interested in his people becoming transformed by God's love than caught up in the act of worshipping him with empty words and actions. Are we not all called to imitate

Christ? And if we are then are we not also called to do more than just imitate his external actions. We are called to be Christ, in every moment and aspect of our lives. In order for that to happen, we need to get ourselves out of the way. We need to get in touch with the God voice that dwells deep within our hearts; the voice that calls each and every one of us to be Christ to one another. We all need to be present to the one that promised to be with us for eternity.

During the days that Christ lived and walked on earth many people such as the Pharisees were considered to be quite knowledgeable about religion and religious affairs. Yet their vast knowledge did not keep them from crucifying our Lord. How much more animosity and killing will we have to endure over whose religion have all the "right" answers to all the divine questions? Where does love fall into this equation of great wisdom and knowledge? Why are we uncomfortable with the mystery that shrouds the Divine? In our God voice there is knowledge, love, healing, forgiveness, wholeness and holiness. Through this voice of love we can experience an awareness and understanding that exists beyond anything that this world can offer to any of us.

We must remember that Christ taught us through his parables. When Jesus answered his Disciples question of why he speaks to the people in parables, he said to them in reply, *"Because knowledge of the mysteries of the kingdom of heaven has been granted to you, but to them it has not been granted?"*

Those that choose to harden their hearts rather than opening them to God's love and message miss the extraordinary dialogue that can occur between a person's heart and God. It is only God who really knows our hearts. He speaks in and through them, and our words and actions reflect our heart's inner motivations and desires. Transformation can only happen when our hearts are set free and beat as one in Christ.

How can we ever forget Jesus' insightful Words of salvation?

*"You shall indeed hear but not*
*Understand,*
*You shall indeed look but never see.*
*Gross is the heart of this people,*
*They will hardly hear with their ears,*
*They have closed their eyes,*
*Lest they see with their eyes*
*And hear with their ears*
*And understand with their heart and*
*Be converted,*
*And I heal them." (Isaiah 6:9-10) (NIV)*

## Scripture Reflections

### Genesis 1:27
*"God Created man in His image;*
*In the divine image he created him;*
*Male and female he created them." (NAB)*

### Galatians 3:28
*God's purpose was to create "one new humanity"*
*as Paul states, "There is neither Jew or Greek,*
*there is neither slave or free, there is no longer male*
*an female; for all of you are one in Christ Jesus."*
*(NAB))*

### John 8:36
*So, Jesus said, "If the Son sets you free you will be*
*free indeed." (NIV)*

### Romans 8:26
*"The Spirit too comes to the aid of our weakness;*
*for we do not know how to pray as we ought but the*
*Spirit itself intercedes with inexpressible groanings."*
*(NAB)*

### 1 Corinthians 3:16
*"Do you not know that you are the temple of God,*
*and that the Spirit of God dwells in you? (NAB)*

Look up each of the following scriptural passages, and using your own words paraphrase each of their messages and tell how they might apply to you in your life and how you should treat others.

**Romans 12: 6-8, 9-10**_____

_____

_____

_____

_____

**Philippians 2:3-5** _____

_____

_____

_____

_____

**Romans 15:3** _____

_____

_____

_____

_____

**2Corinthians 10-12, 13** _____

_____

_____

_____

**1 Peter 4:10-11** _____

_____

_____

_____

_____

**Psalm 33:20**
*"Our soul waits for the Lord; He is our help and our shield."(NAB)*

**Taking it to Heart**

What a remarkable reason to celebrate. You are free to be the special person that God created you to be. All are equal in the eyes of God, all one in Christ. In Ephesians 2: 18-22 it says, *"For through him we both have access in one Spirit to the Father.* *"So then you are no longer strangers and sojourners, but you are fellow citizens with the holy ones and members of the household of God, built upon the foundation of the apostles and prophets, with Christ Jesus himself as the capstone. Through him the whole structure is held together and grows into a temple sacred in the Lord; in him you also are being built together into a dwelling place of God in the Spirit."(NAB)*

Theologian Dietrich Bonhoeffer says it most eloquently, *"God manifests in the connection between two people."* God can show up in our relationships. He is present and visible to us when we are in relationship with others.

**Workbook Questions**

1. What is your story in this Church?

2. Are we not all one body in Christ?

3. How do we as Christians represent the Church?

4. Isn't God an "all inclusive God" loving all people that he created? Where might we find evidence of this in scripture?

5. How might we better represent our Church?

6. How might God want us to live as disciples of his Church?

7. How can we distinguish one person from another? How might God?

8. How can our churches be used as an instrument of God's reconciliation and healing in our hearts?

9. How can our man-made church laws become fences to the unity that Jesus preached?

10. How do we love those who are different from ourselves, or those who don't share our opinions and values?

11. How many of us know the traditions of our religion better than the Word of God? And where in scripture and to who does Jesus discuss such matters?

12. How do you know that you have given your heart to God? Why is it important for you to listen to your heart?

**Prayer Affirmations:**

1. I am made in the image and likeness of God. We are all children of God.

2. God loves me just the way I am which gives me the courage to find it in my heart to love others just the way they are.

3. God help me to forgive those who have hurt me in any aspect of my life.

4. I feel safe to acknowledge my anger and realize that in getting in touch with my emotions it is the first step towards healing and reconciliation.

5. God help me to be an imitator of Jesus in all that I say and do. Assist me in building a Christian community and keep me from those things that can divide it.

## Journaling from the Heart

Share a story of a time or event in your life where you felt others were keeping you out; or a time when you put up a fence/wall to keep someone else out.

_____

_____

_____

_____

_____

_____

_____

_____

_____

_____

_____

_____

_____

_____

_____

_____

_____

_____

_____

_____

_____

_____

_____

# 3

# FENCES THAT HOLD US IN

### Freedom In Sharing With God And Others

J an ~ Somewhere along life's journey we find ourselves
believing that we need to be surrounded by walls or
fences. I often convince myself that they protect me in some
way, by setting up boundaries around my life. I believe that
they will keep out the unwanted truths and harsh realities
of life from getting in. Although these fences harness our
deepest and darkest secrets within our hearts, in doing so
they also keep us from letting others in. It was my daughter's
love for poetry that led me to read Robert Frost's poem entitled, "*Mending Walls.*" The poem speaks of the spring ritual
of mending stone fences in New England. Frost describes
two farming neighbors, who meet in the spring to gather and
mend the stones that have fallen off of the fences between
their lands during the winter. This ritual of "mending" is
ironic because on a deeper level it can prohibit their relationship from growing. The poem reveals that although the
farmers work to keep the fence intact, nature continues to
destroy it just as God works to tear down those personal
fences we erect.

One of the farmers wonders why they even have the
fence, while the other can only respond by saying, "*Good
fences make good neighbors.*" Do good fences really make

good neighbors? I believe that often times they only serve to separate us from one another and eventually it is only the fence that we have in common and our need to sustain it. What is our motivation in building a fence in the first place? Why are we hiding behind fences? What or who are we protecting ourselves from and why? These are the questions that we must find answers to in order to see beyond our fears, and into our hearts trapped behind the fence.

The travel writer Sir Philip Gibbs, in *The Cross of Peace*, wrote:

*"The problem of fences has grown to be one of the most acute that the world must face. Today there are all sorts of zigzag and criss-crossing separating fences running through the races and people of the world. Modern progress has made the world a neighborhood: God has given us the task of making it a brother hood. In these days of dividing walls of race and class and creed we must shake the earth anew with the message of the all-inclusive Christ, in whom there is neither bond nor free, Jew nor Greek, Scythian nor barbarian, but all are one."*

Why do we shut out the people that we need the most, the people with the power to love, serve, and even save us? We often find ourselves choosing forms of communication that entangle us in webs of hostility. Our fences and walls form from our hurtful words spoken out of anger or misunderstanding. How will we ever penetrate the thick walls we have built over time or scale the high fences that rise up before us? Conflicts, both racial and religious in far off countries, should be enough to motivate us to prevent such mistrust and hatred in our own neighborhoods, churches, and homes as well as within our own hearts.

Whenever we choose to put up a wall or build a fence we destroy our relationships with other people. We cut ourselves off from them completely and in turn shut ourselves off from God. He is not content in seeing our lives with out him or with out fellowship. In Christ, we are to be united with all of God's people; for he is all and dwells in all.

## We Are All One Body In Christ

In the September issue of Time Magazine, there is a particular picture which caught my attention. The photograph captures a single moment amidst the chaos known as 9/11. The picture reveals eight people, all running from the destruction and covered in ash from the fall of the Twin Towers. No one face can be distinguished from another, whether black or white, man or woman, Catholic or Protestant. All you can see from the picture are eight different people coming together not only as Americans but as members of one human race, embracing and helping each other to safety. An unknown source later put down in words what this photograph made us feel inside. The words seem to echo Christ's hope for his beloved children.

*"It lifts up the irony that when the great walls of the World Trade Center came crashing down, ironically and miraculously, so did the walls of prejudice, fears, and hatred- As the soot, dirt, and ash rained down upon the people, we became one color. As we carried each other down the stairs of the burning building, we became one class. As we lit candles of hope, we became one generation. As the firefighters and police officers fought their way into the inferno, we became one gender. As we fell to our knees in prayer for strength, we became one faith. As we whispered or shouted words of encouragement, we spoke one*

*language. As we gave our blood in lines a mile long, we became one body. As we mourned together the great loss, we became one family. As we cried tears of grief and loss, we became one soul. And finally as we remember the sacrifices of those who became our heroes, we become one people."*

The events of September 11th united the world but we must remember that every day God calls us to be one gender, one class, one faith, one family, one nation and one body in Christ. Can we not open our hearts as one in Christ to tear down fences and to build bridges of love instead?

## Imprisoned by our Secrets

*Jan* ~ There will always be those life experiences that we would rather not talk about or even remember. True stories of a family secret we have hidden from the rest of the world. We each have our own unfortunate truths that we build fences around to prevent others from learning. There are times when we feel that no one can really understand, for how could they, our life experiences are your own. In these times when we feel most alone, we are often separated from the community and sometimes even from God.

I will never forget the feelings of isolation, fear and sadness that I had experienced as a youth growing up in a turbulent period of uncertainty when my parents struggled to keep their marriage alive and healthy. Our entire family suffered from the traumatic effects that it caused. As a twelve year old growing up in the 60's the word divorce was taboo. I knew of no other family at those times, who were experiencing the ill effects of a broken home. The pain and heartache that I felt as my parents argued alienated me from my friends and isolated me from the rest of my faith community.

Experiencing feelings of both embarrassment and sorrow I felt alone with no one to turn to or share in my experience. My parents were too engaged and drowning in their own world of chaos and pain to even begin to notice my own feelings of confusion and unhappiness. There were even those periods that I questioned where God was in all of this insanity. Fortunately, there were also times when I found that my only solace came in the moments I spent writing out my feelings. Through journaling my words became prayers and I soon no longer felt alone. I stopped bringing my friends over to the house for fear that they would discover the truth or witness an outbreak of an argument. My home no longer resembled a safe and happy place to live. It became a battleground, a secret I was forced to keep inside hiding the truth from the rest of the world.

When my parents decided to separate I felt like I had become a prisoner of a broken home, without a voice in their decision. My brother stayed and lived with my dad during my parent's separation, while my mother took me out to California to live and go to grade school. This event isolated me from everything that I had ever known, my dad, grandparents, school, friends, and church community. Going to school in California was different from what I had experienced growing up in Michigan. Again, I protected myself by not telling anyone the secret that I kept hidden deep inside of my heart. I was too afraid to expose what was happening in my life. I feared that if I did, I would have to accept it as reality. I wasn't mentally ready to give up on our family and the hope of us all reuniting. It is here that I began to understand my need to surrender the pain and my family over to God, and to trust in his will alone. When I realized that I had no control over my parent's lives and decisions; it was only then, that I began to feel a sense of peace inside. I felt better believing and trusting that God was now in control of our situation. God would be the one to direct the course of our lives. All I had to do was to be patient, and wait on the Lord. I continued to persevere in prayer knowing that God knows that we are all going to face trials in our lives; and yet, all he desires is that we ask and seek his counsel, love him, follow his ways and keep our hope alive in him.

When my parents reconciled and decided to reunite our family, I believe that it was on account of an outpouring of God's grace. God had heard my prayers for my parents. He answered them by transforming their hearts and minds which enabled them to heal and work out their differences. I believe that it was, and is only with God's love, grace and intervention that my parents are still married to this day and are celebrating over 60 years of marriage. Today, as I reflect back upon those sad and turbulent times I wish that there had been someone there for me to share what was going on inside of me. Someone to whom I could have voiced my pain who could of really cared about my feelings and what I was experiencing. Little did I realize in the beginning that God was there carrying me all along.

## Building a Bridge to a Broken Heart

Children who experience similar family life scenarios need not experience such heartache alone. God calls us to be there for one another especially in our times of pain and sorrow. Children need to be heard but more importantly to be listened to and comforted. All of us desire to share our stories without being judged or made to feel guilty. Children from dysfunctional homes need counseling just as much as their parents. Their feelings need to be expressed in order for healing to begin, to be affirmed that it is not their fault. They must come to know that God loves them and has not abandoned them. Children need to have resources to turn to; our churches have to be more conscious of the hurting families in our world. The community should reach out and provide whatever assistance each family needs in order to begin the process of healing. We can all help to build the necessary bridges that families need to overcome and mend broken hearts.

Many churches provide programs such as Rainbows for children and parents of divorce. Stephen Ministry, Spiritual Direction, Peer Ministries, and other services are offered to hurting parishioners who need a caring person to talk to and pray with. No matter what our age, or what problems we are facing; God wants us to know that we are never alone. He comes to us through our relationships with others. God can be found in every person who listens, comforts, supports, guides, and loves us. Instead of erecting fences to keep our pain in we need to allow Christ to penetrate through our walls/fences to help us to restore our broken relationships. It is only by God's grace that the hearts of our families can be renewed and transformed. It is only "in Christ" that we can all be united as one family.

## Surrendering to God's Perfect Sovereignty

*Molly* ~ God knows I have difficulty letting go of my own self-sufficiency and need for perfection and control. God wants me to feel the divine grace of salvation, but instead I fight, I play victim, or I hold on. The more complicated I make my desire to hang on; the more difficult is the surrender. But, when I, like a child, take his hand and trust, then I feel the joy and comfort of his peace.

We are freed from the Law as we walk by faith in Jesus Christ. Our freedom from the Law is replaced by the new life of the Spirit (Romans7:1-6). In Romans 5:3 Paul boasts of afflictions. Paul says that afflictions make for endurance, endurance for tested virtue, and tested virtue for hope. He assures us that this hope will not leave us disappointed. Paul says that the hardships of life should teach us patience and strengthen our hope. The reason this hope will not disappoint is because the Holy Spirit dwells in our hearts and infuses into them God's love. This is reiterated in Romans 8:25 when Paul says, *"...hoping for what we can not see means awaiting it with patient endurance,"* he tells us to rejoice in hope. He ties trials to hope. When we have the hope of which Paul speaks we can act with full confidence (Corinthians3:12). We will have the courage to go forward with an inner strength. The veil will be removed and the Spirit of truth will prevail.

When I truly let go, and trust in God's mercy, guidance and grace, I am directed by the Spirit and feel comfortable and at peace with where God is leading my heart. It is reflected not only in my outward disposition, but by the calmness and reassurance I feel on the inside. For Paul then knowing and believing in the word of God is not simply a matter of intellect. As we act on the word through trials and suffering we will come to a deeper knowledge of its truth unveiled in our hearts.

My Mom is a remarkable woman. As a middle-aged woman now looking back, I can sympathize easily with how difficult it must have been for my Mom as a young wife and mother of four. My Dad was an insurance agent and often traveled the entire work week leaving her without a car and handling the day to day happenings of a busy family life. In those days there were no anti-anxiety medications or antidepressants, no regular exercise classes, no MOPS group. Your coping mechanisms were more culturally adapted and in our family relaxation, welcoming, exhaustion, stress, and social outlets usually involved alcohol as the drug of choice. Being dealt the same hand, I am sure I would have followed suit.

As a child, I learned this the hard way. For years my Mom had a drinking problem. Often, after a couple of cocktails at dinner she was not herself. In the morning, my Mom would awaken and would return to normal. She would act as if everything was fine, with a smile on her face singing along to the tunes on the radio. I remained in a state of confusion with mixed emotions, but most of all I felt alone in my pain. It was like living the worst kind of secret when something is wrong in your own home and you can't tell anyone about it. I found myself frustrated with her one moment and loving her the next, but most of all I felt alone in my pain. At the time, I had no idea of the dysfunctional dynamics of alcoholism, and it wasn't until I grew up that I realized my psyche had been scarred. Forgiveness is an odd concept. You want to let go of the old feelings, but they seem to surface at the most unexpected times. For me it was only after years of tears and prayers that my anger and pain began to subside. I wanted to let go, but I couldn't do it on my own, it was God who made the interior change in my heart.

Learning to wait patiently is an important characteristic for us to develop. Each time I admit my sin, and accept forgiveness, my faith and hope has a chance to be exercised and grow stronger. I no longer have to hide in shame every time I slip. I can admit my wrongs and move on. God's love for me is reaffirmed every time I rely on it. In this way, God helps me hold my head high and gives me hope.

I learned what patience is all about when my sisters and I took my Mom on a trip for her 75th birthday. On our last night she fell and broke her shoulder. Instead of going home as planned, my sister and I stayed with her in Florida until she got her shoulder pinned. Then we flew to Cleveland to allow her to have surgery in her home town followed by rehabilitation and healing. This whole ordeal caused my mom great suffering and frustration as it affected her mobility. The accident took away her control and she was difficult to deal with. I tried to understand how God sometimes clips our wings so that we have to relinquish control over to Him. Over the next few weeks more surgeries followed when my mom experienced complications with blood clots.

Through it all my Dad, felt that I was the calming influence as I helped her to remember how much God loves her, and was healing her in many ways. My mom is not a great patient, and during the hospitalization, she experienced withdrawal from her drinking. I wanted to control everything my mom was going through, but I soon realized that only God was in control. I trusted in him, and day by day I remained a comforting and prayerful force in her life as God did in mine. I learned to recognize how to use what I had learned during my own personal struggles with an eating disorder. Jesus may not have taken away my suffering, but I now realized that he had walked with me in my pain, just as he was doing for my mother, and with his help she found a way to get sober and stay that way. By enduring, my mother and I relinquished control and turned our hearts over to God. Soon after my Mom called to say she was reading the gospel passage of the hemorrhaging woman. She said, "*I just cried and said I wish I could touch your cloak too.*" Since that day I have my Mom back. We have had wonderful real conversations about life, our memories, and the spiritual awareness of God's presence in our day to day experiences. It was totally worth waiting for.

**Taking it to Heart**

Instead of building our own fences, Jesus wants us to help him to build his Kingdom, to be members of his household. It was Jesus who came to restore relationships and to comfort the broken hearted. All we have to do is give him our hearts and wait in his Presence.

A Spiritual Reflection by: Macrina Wiederkehr, from (*The Heart's Journey Through the Seasons: The Circle of Life*) with a quote from James Finley from ("The *Awakening Call*").

> "*This is where the union of wills begins—by becoming silent enough to risk experiencing the full weight of this inner touching of the heart and then to base one's entire life upon it....One must step off the edge of the explainable, must risk believing in God, who like an eternal beggar, poorer than poor, waits to find the one who is willing to live for {God} alone. One must risk entering into the silence in which one is brought to say*", "*I am the one for whom God Waits*".

## Scripture Reflections

### Ephesians 2:20-21
*"Built upon the foundation of the apostles and prophets, with Christ Jesus Himself as the cornerstone. In whom the whole structure is joined together And grows into a Holy temple in the Lord."* *(NIV)*

### 2 Corinthians 3:18
*"All of us have had that veil removed so that we can be mirrors that brightly reflect his glory even more. When we trust in Christ for our salvation, he begins to work on the transformation of our hearts, as the Spirit works within us; he changes us to be more and more like Christ."*

Find where in Scripture you see Jesus healing the broken hearted and those in pain? Give examples? Where in the Old Testament do you see God's followers trusting and waiting on God?

_____
_____
_____
_____
_____
_____
_____
_____
_____
_____
_____

Look up and compare the following scripture verses. **1 Peter 1:6-7, Psalm 73:26, James 1:2-4** and **Job 23:8-10.** What do they have in common? How do they speak to our suffering and trials?

_____

_____

_____

_____

_____

_____

_____

_____

_____

_____

_____

_____

_____

_____

_____

_____

_____

_____

_____

_____

_____

_____

_____

_____

_____

### Workbook Questions

1. When in your life did you ever feel alone?

2. Why does God not want us to go through life alone?

3. Why do we put up walls and fences when we are hurting?

4. Where might you put up walls/fences in your life that house hatred, jealousy, resentment or anger?

5. How can Jesus free us from the fences that we construct and those that we choose to hide behind?

6. What secrets do you keep hidden deep within your heart?

7. What is the underlying fear that doesn't allow you to share your pain?

8. Describe a time in your life when you felt like you hit bottom. Were you able to relinquish control? Was God there for you?

9. What was your "ah ha" experience?

## Prayer Affirmations

1. I find comfort and strength in the Lord.

2. God is my refuge in times of trouble.

3. As a mother comforts her child so I will comfort you (Is 66:13)

4. I choose to be patient and wait on the Lord.

5. Make me a vessel of your peace.

6. Be still and know that I am God. (Proverbs)

7. I will follow wherever God leads me.

8. I am safe and secure in God's love.

9. Transformed by God's grace, I am able to forgive.

10. I move forward embraced in God's love.

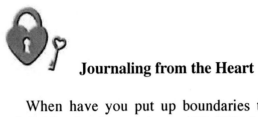

## Journaling from the Heart

When have you put up boundaries to hide something painful that has happen in your life? Maybe it is time to share those deep, painful and buried feelings. Perhaps the opportunity to share or begin to heal is now; to realize that you are not alone, that others have similar experiences, and that God has been there all along just waiting for you to surrender it to him.

_____

_____

_____

_____

_____

_____

_____

_____

_____

_____

_____

_____

_____

_____

_____

_____

_____

_____

_____

_____

# 4

# FENCES BETWEEN OURSELVES &GOD

## Desiring A Relationship With God

*"Every time you don't follow your inner guidance you find a loss of energy, loss of power, a sense of spiritual deadness."*

Shalkti Gaunain

We begin to understand who we are by developing a personal openness and affinity with God. To develop such a rapport with God we need to discover the importance of prayer, scripture, and other spiritual disciplines. Connecting to the Spirit who dwells within your heart is an integral part to both discovering your God voice and your spiritual gifts. In the book, <u>Reason Informed by Faith</u>, by Richard M. Gula S.S., quotes James Gustafson, one of America's leading Protestant ethician who believes that *"Proper doctrine without a passionate relationship to the God whom the doctrine seeks to delineate hardly leads to Christian moral intentions and actions."*

*Jan* ~ God also works through our relationships with family and friends. God is therefore, present and working through our life experiences. What happens in our relationship to God is analogous to what happens when we develop a deep personal relationship with others. For example, my love for my children qualifies my understanding of them and what their well-being requires. My love therefore, affects what I see in my children and how I relate to them and how they respond to me. So when I enter into a relationship with God, his love for me and how well he knows and understands me affects how I am to act in response to that love. In other words, I then can become God's love for others.

## Food for the Soul

To live out our faith, we need nourishment, just as our bodies need food to grow. When we are in union with Christ we are plugged into the source of our spiritual nourishment. Therefore, you ask how do we grow in our relationship with God and mature in our faith? We develop and learn who we are in Christ by seeking. In Jeremiah 29:13 it says, *"You will seek me and find me when you seek me with all your heart."* We grow not by passively watching or being told what to think or how to grow, but by being an active participator, asking questions, searching out answers, expanding our knowledge and enriching our understanding of our faith and God.

In the November 1999 document issued by the American bishops, entitled <u>*Our Hearts Were Burning Within Us,*</u> a title taken from the Emmaus story, the bishops describe three key principal characteristics that can aid us in developing a healthy and mature faith: a *"living faith"*, *"being explicit"*, and *"being fruitful"*. Our world is ever changing therefore it is important that our faith life adapts to those changes without losing its central identity. To keep my faith alive, I need to adjust my spirituality to the changes around me. That does not mean that I give in to the ways of the world that conflict with the teachings of Christ, but it does mean that I find new ways to adapt my faith life to those changing conditions without losing sight of who I am in Christ. Many times that involves meeting people where they are at and loving them as Jesus would have, and yet not compromising my own values to just fit in. *"Living in the world, but not being a part of it."* Instead, I need to be Christ in the world, by finding new ways to set an example of God's love and mercy through both my words and actions.

It is not about holding on to the past, and becoming a prisoner to it, both stagnant and ineffective, it is about *"reading the signs of the times,"* and responding to them in creative and effectual ways. We can always learn from our past and take from it those sacred traditions that are necessary to the essential identity of our faith, but we must be careful to hold loosely those traditions or rituals which no longer provide us with meaning which we can embrace and grow from. Doing anything without the knowledge of why we are doing it holds no meaning for our lives. Nor, does doing something only because that is the way we have always done it necessarily mean that we can apply it to our present lives and experiences. Any spiritual life without meaning is empty and void. Warren Bennis, a University professor and distinguished professor of business has been quoted, "There is a profound difference between information and meaning." Perhaps this is why Jesus addressed the religious leaders of his day so strongly when the Pharisees and teachers of the law came to Jesus from Jerusalem and asked, *"Why do your disciples break the tradition of the elders? They don't wash their hands before they eat,"* and Jesus reply was, *"and why do you break the command of God for the sake of your tradition?'* (Matthew 15:1-3). *"Thus you nullify the word of God for the sake of your tradition"* (Matthew 15:6b).

Knowledge is a key to our growth, we need to know more about God in order to love and serve him. We need to enrich our understanding of God. Many ways in which we can do that is through our prayer life, frequent reading; studying and personal interaction with the word of God. By critically reflecting on God's revelation as it relates to each of our personal lives we can have a better understanding of the God that we serve. All of these steps draw us closer to God and to greater conversion in our faith and love for Christ. Knowledge without a personal relationship with Christ is empty.

I must ask myself *"who is God to me"*? It is in the seeking, in asking the questions, that I probe to find the answers and meaning for my life. I will learn and understand more about my faith and relationship with God when I actively take part in the process; when I turn my doing into being. To be the person God created me to be. If I choose to remain passive and leave all thinking to everyone else I fail to learn what is most important about developing a relationship with God and maturing in my faith. I must *"be explicit"* in my desire to know, love and serve God.

Finally, my faith life must be "fruitful" if I truly desire to be a disciple of Christ. My words and actions must glorify God. My life can no longer just be about me and what I want. I must now seek out God's will; by surrendering my will to become an instrument of his grace. I can then represent God to others and produce a great harvest of goodness for the Lord.

The questions we need to ask are: what are those characteristics about ourselves, things or people that keep us from nurturing our relationship with God? What human made fences do we erect or that we give permission to come between us and God?

## Giving God Access to Our Hearts

Jan ~ When I self-impose the fences in my life, they only serve to limit my relationship with God. In order for me to live by faith without building fences, demands an enormous challenge that begins within my heart. Therefore, I must ultimately choose to allow God greater access to my heart and influence my mind as well. Too often, my mind likes to play tricks by telling me that there are no fences that stand between me and my relationship with God. Yet, the heart yearns to reveal to me the truth.

When I think of how many fences or barriers I build that keep me from God's access and influence I feel embarrassed and ashamed. Barriers of anger, fear, selfishness, pride, and self righteousness stifle my growth. It seems that I can only approach God with true honesty and humility when my heart is made open. Many times I feel closest to God in times of brokenness. It is when I am experiencing great trials and suffering that I hear God's voice the loudest. Other times, I am caught up in the things of this world, and the busyness of daily living. Life can capture us in a whirlwind of activity where the noise and confusion drowns out our communication with God. It is in these times that I can barely even hear him whisper. Some times I find my inner voice shouting, *"Stop the World I want to get off."* Something deep inside of my heart is instructing me to stop the madness, to be still and know that God is there. He is waiting for me to surrender my whole heart to him so I can experience a joy and peace beyond all understanding.

## Being Brought to Our Knees

*Jan* ~ I will never forget the time in my life when I felt the pull of the world and all of life's busyness taking me away from time spent with God. Family life can be filled with people moving in different directions, work, school, volunteer and church work, extended family commitments, friends, social gatherings, housework, and homework, yard work, preparing meals, grocery shopping, the laundry, paying bills, and playing taxi driver. Then when daily living isn't enough to keep you from finding time to connect to God, an injury stops you dead in your tracks, adding pain and frustration to your pile. Now not only are you behind on what you should be doing, you feel guilty about taking time out to heal physically, emotionally, mentally and spiritually.

In the midst of a particularly stressful year when I needed my family to pitch in and help, my husband had a terrible accident. He fell off a ladder, destroying his knee to the point that he was confined to a wheelchair for months. He needed surgery and missed six months of work. I was barely finishing my own physical therapy, still hurting from a back and neck injury when we received news that my father in law had a heart attack. Shortly thereafter, my mother in law had a stroke. Immediately, I needed to resume my role as caregiver, taking on and off various hats as I played taxi, ambulance driver, nurse, counselor, wife, mother, and friend.

When I look back I can remember that it was somewhere between being forced flat on my back and my husband's injuries, that I realized something. I no longer had the strength to do it on my own. I needed to surrender, to ask for God's help, to believe that he would see me through the pain and suffering. I had always known somewhere deep within my heart that I could call upon God; to ask him to take control of my life. However, it wasn't until God brought me to my knees, through the collapsing of the world around me that I knew that I needed to *"let go and let God"* be the director of my life. In the Gospel of Matthew 11:28-30 Jesus says, *"Come to me, all you who are weary and burdened, and I will give you rest. Take my yoke upon you and learn from me, for I am gentle and humble in heart, and you will find rest*

*for your souls. For my yoke is easy and my burden is light."*
My burden was far too heavy for me to carry alone. My heart
was crying out to the Lord and God heard and answered my
plea.

Never could I have imagined that our whole family
would continue to suffer as the world unraveled before us.
I prayerfully watched as each of my family members were
deeply affected by the life- changing events that were taking
place in our lives. God continued to call each of them out,
bringing them to their knees.

It was my husband, Ken, who resisted the most. With
each prayer of petition that I offered up to God, it seemed
that he only held on more firmly, seeking to control his life.
Through each obstacle that he endured, every surgery, and
complication I prayerfully stood by. I remember bringing
him a plaque to adorn his sterile hospital room which read,
*"My grace is sufficient for you, for my power is made perfect
in weakness"* (2 Corinthians 12:9). Slowly, I watched him
give over his control to God.

That Bible verse became a cornerstone of strength for
our family that year. What we didn't realize back then was
that the Holy Spirit was preparing us for an even greater
battle. God knew each of our hearts. He knew we needed to
be in relationship with him if we were ever going to make it
through the suffering which was about to take place. A year
of injuries and hospitalizations ended when we lost both of
Ken's parents within five days of each other. His dad died
on my daughter, Lauren's 18th birthday and my mother in
law died unexpectedly only days thereafter. As difficult as
it was for all of us to deal with none of us felt alone. God
carried each of us through the funerals and long after he is
still carrying us. Even the death of those closest to us could
not keep us from God's love. We who are believers are co-
heirs with Christ, Romans 8:16-17 says, *"The Spirit himself
testifies with our spirit that we are God's children."* Now

if we are children, then we are heirs—heirs of God and co-heirs with Christ, if indeed we share in his sufferings in order that we may also share in his glory. That year it was through all of our pain and suffering that we drew closer in our relationship to God. He used all of our suffering to bear witness to others his power and glory given to the faithful.

## God Hungers to be in Relationship with Us

*Jan~* I know that it is through God's grace that the Holy Spirit awakened faith in me, and that the new life is to know the Father and the one whom he has sent, Jesus Christ. *(Jn 17:3).* Our desire to know God is a gift of the Spirit, and God's call is placed deep within our hearts. The hunger that we feel is the same hunger that God feels for us. He needs us to respond to the love that he has already given us.

St. Teresa of Avila encourages us to hold conversations with Christ. She tells us that *"meditation is not a monologue, but rather a dialogue."* Even when we think that God is being silent, he is speaking clearly to our hearts. When our hearts plead him to do so he is there. The closer we draw to the Lord the more we know in our hearts that he has heard us.

Sometimes, we should ask ourselves why? Why do I continue to erect fences that keep my relationship with God from developing and deepening? Why do I allow the sin in my life and in the world to sabotage my relationship with God? First, by being aware of my sins or personal fences this will help me to begin the process of tearing them down. Secondly, seeking reconciliation and forgiveness from God and those whom I have hurt will also open up my heart. Finally, in finding my God voice, I will draw closer to God and others through his grace. The more we learn to lead with the eyes of our hearts the better disciples we will become and the more productive we will be in building up God's Kingdom.

When we pray, we are actually saying I want to have a relationship with God. Relationships develop through a process. When we look at our own friendships or the love for our spouses,' we can easily reflect on the stages of that experience; so it is with our spiritual relationship with God.

## God is in All Things and in Everyone We Meet

*Molly* ~ When I first met Jan we sat next to each other at an introductory session of our Masters program. We exchanged information about a recent ministry position that we had both applied for, and found to our amazement that it was for the same job. This initial stage is what Fr. Thomas Keating entitles *"acquaintanceship."* Whether with my friend, Jan or my relationship with God, in the beginning there is an element of formality and awkwardness, but it is also informational in nature. We are getting acquainted. In prayer, it might be expressed so that we stay in contact with this spiritual dimension. We might say Grace before meals, attend Church, a Bible study, or Sunday school, or maybe recite the *"Our Father"*.

As Jan and I got to know each other it became much more informal to exchange thoughts, and ideas in conversation. There was a definite comfort level involved. We shared more details of our personal stories and found many commonalities. It was great realizing that we had grown up in the Detroit area around the same time, moved to Grand Rapids and surprisingly enough even married men that had attended the same Catholic high school.

In our prayer life, as we grow more comfortable interacting with God, we become more open to allowing him to impact our lives and spirits. We might feel God's presence in nature, or when reading Scripture, his message suddenly comes alive and we have one of those "ah ha" moments where we feel a certain passage speaks directly to our hearts.

As Jan and I became true friends we were more available to each other, disclosed more of our inner selves and were committed to our journey together. There was a definite spontaneity where we could share our joys, and sadness, laugh, cry, and just be ourselves with one another. Trust was established and we often talk to each other daily.

I believe "friendship" is where our hearts can be converted. Somehow, this special person has resonated in the deep recesses of our being and you know that God has blessed you with a great gift. So too, does this occur in our spiritual lives. Our response is one of gratitude in which our hearts, feelings, and emotions are open to our connectedness with our "Abba". Prayer becomes much more frequent and spontaneous.

The final stage of growth in a relationship is considered "intimacy". With Jan, I found I could just pick up the phone and without uttering a word she could sense how my day was going. She accepted me warts and all and didn't expect me to act or be a certain way. She was more then just a friend she became like a soul-mate who understood my heart.

In prayer, if we have an intimate and personal relationship we have arrived at a contemplative posture. We notice God in all things, and in everyone we meet. We can just lie in God's arms, embraced by a decidedly knowing understanding of unconditional love. Ahhhh....

## Reclaiming your God Voice

*Molly* ~ Life is our opportunity to test our faith and meet God in these never ending prayer moments. For me mid-life has propelled me to the depths and challenged me to intimately trust in the Presence of God who dwells within me and to let go of much of what I had known. Menopause took me quite by surprise. I had always thought I was fairly in touch with my body. But at the young age of 43, my periods stopped completely. I was thrown into a hormonal nightmare where I literally felt like an alien had taken over my body. All semblance of control had slipped away without any acquiescence on my part. The grief over the finality of my infertility was deep and profound, but in its despair I realized we give birth in many ways. For me the grace came in understanding that to move forward I had to embrace the experience and reclaim my voice. Julian of Norwich challenges us to what she identifies as the *"sweet touchings"* of grace.

*"And so we shall by his sweet grace in our own meek continual prayer come in him in this life by many sweet touchings of sweet spiritual sights and feelings measured out to us as our simplicity may bear it." (Julian of Norwich Showings L43, 255). Someone once said to me "woman must come of age by herself...she must find her true center alone."*

At fifty, I found myself processing this whole salvific plan on a more personal level, so that I could grow in communion with God. Only then can I fully engage as a woman that is authentic to the calling God has designed for me. There is a wonderful poem entitled *"The Call"* by Oriah Mountain Dreamer that begins:

*I have heard it all my life,*
*A voice calling a name I recognize as my own.*
*Sometimes it comes as a soft-bellied whisper,*
*Sometimes it holds an edge of urgency.*
*But always it says: Wake up, my love. You are walking*
*    asleep.*
*There's no safety in that!*
*Remember what you are and let this knowing*
*Take you home to the Beloved with every breath...*

If salvation is about an inner epiphany, then by accepting myself in freedom before God, I am drawing closer to my true-self and in so doing developing a deeper union with him. When I acknowledge God in all things, God instills in me a sense of direction. I think that is what mid-life and menopause has been about for me. It has taken me out of the world for a while. It has taken me away from a focus outside of self to my inner turmoil and need for approval. Jung talks about this idea that the works you do in the first half of your life are not necessarily the works you do in the second. But I would not have been able to effectively reach out to others until I had gone inward. All my questioning, searching, experiencing and conversations have been part of God's plan to lead me to this very moment in time. I have been given the freedom to choose. I must respect and honor that freedom. God is in control. I am not. For me that is where it all began. Do not be afraid. God is utterly trustworthy. I have assurance of God's presence in my life. It is such a humbling thought. I see now how it makes me a more compassionate minister and allows me to be present to others.

I recounted earlier the beginning of the poem, *"The Call"*; I would like to close with the last stanzas:

*Hold tenderly who you are, and let a deeper knowing*
*Color the shape of your humanness.*
*There is nowhere to go. What you are looking for is right*
*   here.*
*Open the fist clenched in wanting and see what you*
*   already hold in your hand.*
*There is no waiting for something to happen,*
*No point in the future to get to,*
*All you have ever longed for is right here in this moment,*
*   right now.*
*You are wearing yourself out with all this searching.*
*Come home and rest.*

*How much longer can you live like this?*
*Your hungry spirit is gaunt; your heart stumbles. All this*
    *trying.*
*Give it up!*
*Let the Lover pull you to your feet and hold you close,*
*Dancing even when fear urges you to sit this one out.*
*Remember there is one word you are here to say with*
    *your whole being.*
*When it finds you, give your life to it. Don't be tight-*
    *lipped and stingy.*
*Spend yourself completely on the saying.*
*Be one word in this great love poem we are writing*
    *together.*
Oriah Mountain Dreamer

**Taking it to Heart**

Living every moment in relationship with God should be our destiny, it is what our hearts were created for; to be wrapped in the arms of our Savior's love and be changed by it. Salvation comes when two hearts beat as one; it comes in the surrender, in the giving of your heart to Christ, and in dying to self and waiting on the Lord. Come home, says the Lord, and let your heart rest in me.

## Scripture Reflections

Which of the following Scripture passages most resonate with you? Write in your own words how each of the passages speaks to your heart.

**Psalm 46:10** *"Be still and know that I am God."(NIV)*

_____

_____

_____

_____

_____


**Galatians 4:9** *"Now, however, that you know God, or rather to be known by God, how can you turn back"(NAB)*

_____

_____

_____

_____

_____


**Isaiah 55:6** *"Seek the Lord while He may be found, call upon Him while He is near."(NIV)*

_____

_____

_____

_____

_____

**Jeremiah 29:13** *"Now therefore; reform your ways and your deeds; listen to the voice of the Lord your God, so that the Lord will repent of the evil with which he threatens you."* _____

_____

_____

_____

_____

**Matthew 11:28-30** *"Come to me, all you who labor and are burdened, and I will give you rest. Take my yoke upon you and learn from me, for I am meek and humble of heart, and you will find rest for yourselves. For my yoke is easy, and my burden light."* _____

_____

_____

_____

_____

**2 Corinthians 12:9** *"My grace is sufficient for you, for power is made perfect in weakness."* _____

_____

_____

_____

_____

**Romans 8:16-17** *"The Spirit itself bears witness with our spirit that we are children of God. And if children, then heirs, heirs of God and joint heirs with Christ, if only we suffer with him so that we may also be glorified with him.* _____

_____

_____

_____

_____

**3** *"Now this is eternal life: that they should know you, the only true God, and the one whom you sent, Jesus Christ."* _____

_____

_____

_____

_____

**Workbook Questions**

1. What keeps you from having a deeper relationship with God?

2. What do you need to do to surrender your life to God?

3. How does God work through other people in your life in order to get your attention?

4. What does a relationship with God mean to you? What would it look like? How would you describe your relationship with God this very moment?

5. What is the key to your growth as a Christian? How might you better understand God? What is God revealing to you right now?

6. What must you do to strengthen your faith life?

7. When do you hear God calling you the loudest? How do you respond?

8. What might you do to help others to grow in their relationship with God?

**Prayer Affirmations**

1. It is the heart always that sees, before the head can see. *Thomas Carlyle*

2. I am God's expression of life. Right where I am right now I can love myself.

3. The Past is behind me. I forgive myself.

4. I am a child of God protected and surrounded by love.

5. I accept God's guidance and direction. I am safe.

6. God supports me. I am wonderful.

7. God operates at every level of my life. All is well.

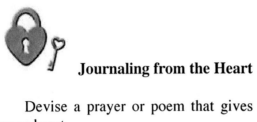

## Journaling from the Heart

Devise a prayer or poem that gives God all access to your heart.

_____

_____

_____

_____

_____

_____

_____

_____

_____

_____

_____

_____

_____

_____

_____

_____

_____

_____

_____

_____

_____

_____

# 5

# FENCES OF ENVY

### Accepting and Loving Ourselves as Children of God

*A heart at peace gives life to the body, but envy rots the bones. (Proverbs14:30 NIV)*

It has been said that envy not only wants what another person has, it also wants the other person not to have it. The word (phthonos) was the Greek word for envy. Euripides, the writer of Greek Tragedies called it "the greatest of all diseases among men." The very essence of the word does not describe a spirit which desires nobly or dishonorably, to have what someone else has. Sadly, the word describes an embittered spirit which grudges the fact that the other person has these things at all. The Stoics defined it as "grief of someone else's good." St. Basil called it "grief at your neighbor's good fortune."

The word "zelos" from which our word zeal comes from was originally considered a good word. It meant "emulation," the desire to attain to nobility when we see it. Unfortunately, it was reduced to and became known as the desire to have what someone else has. When God instructed the Israelites in the desert, he paid special attention to envy, commanding them, *"You shall not covet your neighbor's wife. You shall not set your desire on your neighbor's house or land, his manservant or maidservant, his ox or donkey, or anything that belongs to your neighbor"* (Deuteronomy 5:20–22). Cain killed his brother for the same reason that people today in our culture kill because of jealousy and envy. Joseph's brothers made a similar attempt. Jacob and Esau, Sarah and Hagar, David and Saul—the Bible is rife with stories of envy and strife.

We may not go as far as doing away with those towards whom we exhibit feelings of envy or jealousy, but those emotions can intrude themselves into our lives. We begin to harbor feelings of righteousness and resentment toward those that have what we believe we deserve. When these emotions go unbridled they can turn us into green eyed monsters. This envious monster's venom will not only be unleashed on those we are envious of but, will ultimately turn inward, poisoning our very being by drawing us further away from God and our true selves.

## The Green Eyed Monster

*Jan* ~ I remember when my children were quite young and they were both invited to a birthday party of a friend in the neighborhood. I offered to help out at the party. The mother had just recently had a new baby and I knew that escorting rambunctious eight year olds to Chucky Cheese while caring for a new born might be more than she could handle. Immediately she took up my offer.

After all of the presents had been unwrapped and everyone had finished their last piece of cake, and their final jump in the ball cage, I helped round up all of the birthday participants. I packed up the van with the presents and made a final head count to ensure we had not forgotten anybody.

Everyone seemed to have a great time at the party and each of the children received a balloon for attending the party by Chucky Cheese himself. Once everyone was in the van, balloons and all, we looked like a circus act rolling out of town.

It wasn't long after we left the restaurant that I began to hear the sounds of crying and arguing children from the back of the van. My neighbor, who happened to be driving seemed to be oblivious to it and continued talking to me. As the sounds of distress increased I could not help but turn my attention to what was occurring in the back of the van. It appeared to me that each of the children were unwillingly handing their balloons over to the birthday girl who was demanding them. With every balloon that she had snatched out of someone's hands the child expressed words of disapproval and tears of sadness. Not wanting to reprimand my neighbor's daughter in front of her, I decided I would ask the children what was happening to make them so upset. Each of them simultaneously, blurted out that the birthday girl was demanding that they give up their balloons because it was her birthday and not theirs. I remember thinking to myself how selfish she was behaving, especially, after having received so many wonderful birthday presents.

To this day, I have never forgotten her mother's reply to her daughter as she looked through the rear view mirror while driving that night. She said, *"Honey, give the kids back their balloons and mommy will make it up to you when we get home."* It probably would not have made such an impact on me as it did that night, had the mother handled the situation more appropriately; but from that day on, I began to understand why the daughter continued to act out as she did in countless other situations. Times when she demanded to have things her way as though she deserved it. It was as though no matter how much she was given it was never enough. She always wanted more of what others had. If she couldn't have it, then nobody could.

Sadly, I believe that much of her feelings of envy had been programmed into her from a very early age. Each time her parents gave in it made the behavior acceptable. Unfortunately, the "green eyed monster" of envy has a way of showing up in many of our lives again and again whether we want him to or not.

## Finding Contentment

When we think of what the opposite of envy might be we are drawn to the word contentment. In 1Timothy 6:6-7 it says, *"True religion with contentment is great wealth. After all, we didn't bring anything with us when we came into the world, and we certainly cannot carry anything with us when we die."* This passage makes sense if we are speaking about being envious of material things, but what about those attributes, gifts, talents, and abilities that others have that I don't? What happens when we become envious or jealous of another's talents or gifts?

The fence of envy or jealousy is an obstacle that we so often self-erect. It keeps us from the freedom of true contentment and peace. When we are always comparing ourselves to others instead of seeing how wonderfully God made us to be, we miss who we truly are in Christ. 2 Peter 1:3 says, *"As we know Jesus better, his divine power gives us everything we need for living a godly life. He has called us to receive his own glory and goodness!"* When we have Jesus Christ, that is all we need, that is all any of us needs.

Christ teaches us how to discern the valuable things in life from those that are only distractions. Our freedom comes in being in Christ's presence, never from accumulating worldly possessions or from being envious of what someone else has or is. Instead of us trying to compare ourselves to others we need to focus on imitating and following Christ.

In Psalm 112: 1-4 it says, *"Praise the Lord! Happy are those who fear the Lord. Yes, happy are those who delight in doing what he commands. Their children will be successful everywhere; an entire generation of godly people will be blessed. They themselves will be wealthy, and their good deeds will never be forgotten. When darkness overtakes the godly, light will come bursting in. They are generous, compassionate and righteous."* God is the only one that can give us true success. No talent, or title, or worldly possession is more steadfast than God's grace and the inheritance that he promises all of us who love and obey him.

## God Doesn't Call the Equipped He Equips the Called

There is an old poem entitled <u>The Master's Touch</u>, by Myra Brooks Welch and this inspirational piece relays a very important message to all of us who work at building a fence of envy around our lives. The poem goes like this:

*'Twas battered and scarred, and the auctioneer*
*Thought it scarcely worth his while*
*To waste much time on the old violin,*
*But held it up with a smile.*
*"What am I bidden, good folks," he cried,*
*"who'll start the bidding for me?"*
*"A dollar, a dollar. Then two! Only two?*
*Two dollars, and who'll make it three?"*
*Three dollars, once; three dollars, twice;*
*Going for three..." But no,*
*From the room, far back, a grey-haired man*
*Came forward and picked up the bow;*
*Then wiping the dust from the old violin,*
*And tightening the loosened strings,*

*He played a melody pure and sweet,*
*As a caroling angel sings.*

*The music ceased, and the auctioneer,*
*With a voice that was quiet and low,*
*Said: "what am I bid for the old violin?"*
*And he held it up with the bow.*
*"A thousand dollars, and who'll make it two?*
*Two thousand! And who'll make it three?*
*Three thousand, once; three thousand, twice,*
*And going and gone," said he.*

*The people cheered, but some of them cried,*
*We do not quite understand...*
*What changed its worth? Swift came the reply:*
*"The touch of the Master's hand."*
*And many a man with life out of tune,*
*And battered and scarred with sin,*
*Is auctioned cheap to the thoughtless crowd*
*Much like the old violin.*

*A "mess of pottage," a glass of wine,*
*A game—and he travel on.*
*He is "going" once, and "going twice,*
*He's "going" and almost "gone."*
*But the master comes, and the foolish crowd*
*Never can quite understand*
*The worth of a soul and the change that is wrought*
*By the touch of the Master's hand.*

Too often we feel like the worn out violin that we think
no longer has any worth. We long to be like the new violins
that garnish a high price tag and attract the crowds. The short
poem shows us that *"our life is more accurately measured
by the lives that we touch than by the things we acquire."* It

reminds us, that *"God doesn't call the equipped, He equips the called."* The old violin in the poem is seen to have worth only after it has been touched by the Master's hand. Just owning a violin doesn't produce beautiful music, it is God's gift to the musician that allows him to produce the beautiful music; music which gives meaning and beauty to the violin. We have all been given special gifts from God. The answer lies in discerning those gifts and using them to build up His kingdom here on earth. Wanting more things, like a new and shiny violin, or desiring what someone else has, such as more musical ability or talent causes resentment and anger when someone has what you thought you deserved. This outlook can only lead to an unhappy and unfulfilled life of endless wanting and emptiness. It is only in the discovery and use of our own unique and spiritual gifts that we ever find true contentment, fulfillment, and peace. All of our gifts together make up the Body of Christ; we are all needed in accomplishing God's mission.

The incredible part of life's journey is when you believe in God, the real desires of your heart are already within you, waiting to be unlocked, waiting to be heard. Your God voice knows what is best for you, for you are someone special, wonderfully made for God's purpose. All you need to do is to find it, discover it, and use it.

In another version of <u>The Master's Touch</u>, a young boy attending a concert with his mother finds his way on stage before the curtain opens without his mother's knowledge. When the curtains are drawn he is seated at the concert piano playing "Twinkle Twinkle Little Star." His mother panics until she notices the concert pianist peacefully appearing on stage. He accompanies her son by placing each of his arms around the young boys shoulder. The concert pianist whispers in the boy's ear *"continue to play and never quit."* Much to the mother's astonishment, her young son and the concert pianist produce beautiful music together. Just like the boy in the story we will not be left alone, God's arms are around us and his hands are there, helping us turn our feeble attempts into a true masterpiece. God will use our desires to produce his good. Our selfish desires will no longer drain our hearts with feelings of envy and jealousy. Through the help of our God voice, our hearts will be filled with a new found joy and peace. We will begin to see our self as God sees us. We will begin to experience the heart of God that lies deep within us. Mother Teresa said it so powerfully, *"We are all pencils in the hand of God."* Being in touch with our God voice allows us with the help of God's grace to create God's wonderment.

### Sharing our voice

*Molly* ~ I used to envy my two sisters and how well they handle both their personal and professional lives. They adapt easily to change and go with the flow with utmost grace and courage. They have always been my most ardent supporters and so encouraging of my being true to my authentic voice even though by the world's standards my journey does not look as "successful."

As an introvert, I regained my strength and energy by periods of quiet and stillness. If I do not have this time away and also moments between projects during the day, I become exhausted, crabby, and withdrawn. If I do take that time to regroup and recharge I am able to feel productive and calm.

My sisters are beautiful extroverts. For them, their energy is fueled by being around and engaged with others. They can go from morning until night and be as available and congenial until their heads hit the pillow with the television blaring.

As I have matured I have appreciated our uniqueness as individuals. The gift I believe is in knowing ourselves and how we can best serve the Kingdom. So moving forward for some of us or waiting or testing our boundaries are all part of God's plan for us to be actively engaged in relationship with him. And in the process we learn a lot about ourselves...

I was certain that when I went into the discernment weekend to choose a focus area for my graduate work that it was a waste of time. I already knew my focus area Ecology and Religion. It seemed perfect. I had been a huge advocate of environmental justice and my spiritual direction practice is very involved in a holistic spirituality. I thought combining the two would lead to a retreat center position in which I could encourage the healing process by being one with God and the earth. But the process was an eye opener. When I went off by myself to pray I found it difficult to stay with a balance between reason and affection. I read over the descriptions of all the other areas and then went on a long walk. I needed to explore other options. I repressed the thoughts and feelings that began to well up. I was very anxious, my stomach was knotted, and I felt like I wanted to run away.

When I clarified it out loud I was amazed how strongly I felt committed to break open Spirituality for Ministry and to delve deeper into many of the readings I had been exposed to in the Spiritual Direction Practicum. It was too much to ignore. Wilke Au expressed it well when he described the balance between affection and intellect (<u>By Way of the Heart</u>). My intellect was saying one thing, my gut reaction was endorsing quite another. I was out of balance. The feeling was very real in my head and in my body. It wasn't until I said it aloud that I realized I was not in agreement. I had come so far on this journey by letting God lead me. I needed to sit with this and wait for the Spirit to guide me. Once I got quiet, I saw how both of those areas affected my body. The ecology piece looked attractive on the outside but when I read the materials and what was expected, it did not feel other-centered. When I checked out how I felt when I read over the spirituality area I literally could feel my body relax and I looked forward to the materials and excited by the opportunity to grow both personally and as a Spiritual Director to others. I recalled how my perfectionist, pleaser nature had again reared its head. I had to be authentic to my own voice. I had to trust that God was in control and I needed to be true to the nudging of the Spirit. It was a wonderful opportunity to experience first hand the discernment piece, and a great learning tool to bring to my practice when others are discerning God's will for their lives.

Discernment is tricky. Not every movement within our hearts can be trusted. To the degree our hearts are moving toward the desire to love and serve God and others, I believe I am under the influence of the Holy Spirit. To the degree they are moving away from this desire, I am not. Desire is central to discernment. It is a more reliable criterion than feelings or inner peace. My feelings change but I still desire to serve, and the direction towards love is also critical. Awareness of the quality of heart underlying my daily actions is the key to daily discernment. Normally when I am moving towards the desire to love and serve God and others, I will experience a quality of heart marked by the fruits of the Spirit – love, joy, peace, patience, etc. When I am moving away from the desire to love and serve I experience a quality of heart marked by inner restlessness and anxiety. My heart is no longer aligned with my deepest self and so I experience disorientation. In short the key to discerning the presence or absence of the Spirit is awareness of my mood. A quality of the heart marked by anxiety is a red flag telling me that something is amiss and should be checked out. The anxiety can be a grace because it calls me to look at my heart and realign it with the Holy Spirit. The Spirit is at work within our consciousness. The crux for learning the skill of discernment of spirits is becoming aware of the situations causing my bad moods. Then I will not fall into the trap of undermining my desire to love and serve others. This understanding has enhanced my ministry as a spiritual director.

I would describe my role as a spiritual director as the art of contemplative listening. It is the gift of helping others to be more responsive to the prompting of the Spirit guiding them in the experiences and relationships of their everyday lives and bringing these experiences to prayer, it is a safe, non-judgmental place where the spiritual aspects of the directee's being can gently unfold. It is intentional and structured. It focuses on a person's faith journey. Several things happen in spiritual direction. Listening is the most important. Not just with ears but with the heart. Clarifying one's God-image is another. In other words, allowing God to be truly real to the directee's. I try to affirm them often, and challenge them in order that they might uncover any areas of hindered and restrictive freedom in their lives. Discernment is a major priority. What is God calling me to do? Many give up when traveling through rough passages. To walk with them where they are even in the midst of the desert is truly spiritual companionship. My challenge in this is not only to hear their voices and the words, but also to listen for reoccurring themes and attend to the silences. I need to pay attention to what is being said beyond words. Not moving them forward or backward but just to trust that God is intimately involved in our daily experience.

## Scripture Reflections

### Ecclesiastes 5:10-12,15 (NCV)

*Whoever loves money*
*will never have enough money;*
*Whoever loves wealth*
*will not be satisfied with it.*
*This also is useless.*

*The more wealth people have,*
*The more friends they have to help spend it.*
*So what do people really gain?*
*They gain nothing except to look at*
*Their riches.*

*Those who work hard sleep in peace;*
*It is not important if they eat little or much.*
*But rich people worry about their wealth*
*and cannot sleep.*

*People come into this world with nothing,*
*and when they die they leave with nothing.*
*In spite of all their hard work*
*they leave just as they came.*
*Then I observed that most people are motivated to*
*success by their envy to their*
*neighbors. But this, too, is meaningless, like*
*chasing the wind."*

### Philippians 4:11-13, 19 (NIV)

*"I am not saying this because I am in need, for I have*
*learned to be content whatever the circumstances. I*

*know what it is to be in need, and I know what it is to have plenty. I have learned the secret of being content in any and every situation, whether well fed or hungry, whether living in plenty or in want. I can do everything through him who gives me strength.... And my God will meet all your needs according to his glorious riches in Christ Jesus.*

### James 3:14-16 (NIV)
*"But if you harbor bitter envy and selfish ambition in your hearts, do not boast about it or deny the truth. Such "wisdom" does not come down from heaven but is earthly, unspiritual, of the devil. For where you have envy and selfish ambition, there you find disorder and every evil practice."*

### 1 Corinthians 3:3 (NIV)
*"You are still worldly. For since there is jealousy and quarreling among you, are you not worldly? Are you not acting like mere men?"*

### Galatians 5:26 (NIV)
*"Let us not become conceited, provoking and envying each other."*

### Exodus 20:17 (NIV)
*"You shall not covet your neighbor's house. You shall not covet your neighbor's wife, or his manservant or maidservant, his ox or donkey, or anything that belongs to your neighbor."*

### 1 Peter 2:1(NIV)
*"Therefore, rid yourselves of all malice and all deceit, hypocrisy, envy, and slander of every kind."*

**John 13:34 (NIV)**
*"A new command I give you: Love one another. As I have loved you, so you must love one another."*

How do the following Scripture passages reflect that God is all we need to satisfy us?

**Proverbs 23:17**

_____
_____
_____
_____
_____

**Hebrews 13:5**

_____
_____
_____
_____

**2 Peter 1: 3**

_____
_____
_____
_____

**Psalm 37:1, 7; 73:25-26**

_____
_____
_____
_____

### Workbook Questions

1. Have you ever felt envious or jealous of someone? Why do you think you felt such feelings? How might you overcome such feelings?

2. How might you help someone that you care about surrender such feelings of envy and jealousy?

3. Does anything good ever come out of being jealous or envious of someone or what someone has?

4. What does jealousy and envy do to undermine your relationships?

5. How might you get passed such feelings of envy and jealousy? What can you do, whom can you turn to, to help you with these negative feelings?

6. What do you think would be the opposite of feeling jealous?

7. Have you ever had someone be jealous or envious of you or what you had? How did that make you feel? How might you have made that person feel better about themselves?

8. What does God say about being jealous or envious about other people and their possessions?

9. What are the special gifts that God has given you? How do you discern what those gifts are? And how can you better use them to fulfill God's Kingdom?

10. How might you help others to discern their special gifts from God?

**Taking it to Heart**

Envy and jealousy do not reflect a spirit of God, but only a spirit of grief and embitterment. Allow God's love to fill up the empty places in your life. Turn your wanting into receiving God's grace and fullness. There is a song by Barlow Girl which is entitled "Enough." It basically exemplifies how Christ is all that anyone of us really needs. God satisfies us....God is Enough!

**Prayer Affirmations**

**Be creative and draw a picture below of what it looks and feels like when all you need to fill you up is God!**

1. God is all I need, and he will satisfy me.

2. I must love others as God has loved me

3. I am content in the gifts that God has given me

4. I can find contentment even when others are prosperous because of my Love for Christ.

5. Godliness with contentment is great gain. *"Tell the rich in the present age not to be proud and not to rely on so uncertain a thing as wealth but rather on God, who richly provides us with all things for our enjoyment." (1 Timothy 6:17 NAB)*

6. Riches in heaven are better than riches on earth.

7. My security is not found in possessions but in God alone.

8. I trust in the Lord for God is always faithful.

9. God can and does use ordinary people like me.

10. Success is about touching the lives of other people for Christ.

11. My fruit is better than fine gold; what I yield surpasses choice silver (Proverbs 8:18-19 NIV)

12. To be successful is to be used by God to do God's work.

**Journaling from the Heart**

Explain an experience in your life when you were filled with envy. How did you feel? What did you do? How did it resolve itself? How did you find peace and contentment?

_____

_____

_____

_____

_____

_____

_____

_____

_____

_____

_____

_____

_____

_____

_____

_____

_____

_____

_____

_____

_____

_____

_____

_____

_____

_____

# 6

# FENCES OF ANGER

### Healing and Reconciliation

*Man's anger does not bring about the righteous life*
*that God desires. James 1:20 NIV*

Anger is one of those fences that wear many masks. We all deal with the emotion of anger, but how we manage it differs from person to person. We as women all too often suppress this emotion by allowing it to personify itself in many different extremes. The children don't pick up their clothes; your husband doesn't call to say he will home late, a friend cancels at the last minute; your boss blames you for his mistake, co-workers gossip about others at the office, or your parent's only brag about their successful child. All of these scenarios can leave you feeling anxious, harboring grudges toward the people in your life. These negative feelings can easily trigger your coping mechanisms and often manifest themselves in non-productive and self destructive behaviors. Some of us over eat, over spend, fall into depression, spread rumors, lash out, or worst of all turn our anger inward and lose our authentic voice.

## Good Girls Don't Get Angry

Anger, a sense of diminishment, a repression of feelings often leads to an abscess of anger. Many let their anger control them and find themselves lost in an abyss of depression and isolation. Healing occurs when emotions surface and are confronted with compassion, forgiveness and grace. Anger can come at us out of nowhere. Physically, we might feel it in our body; some grind their teeth, their muscles tense, a stomach ache may develop or a migraine may ensues followed by a myriad of other symptoms that can overwhelm us. We might find ourselves taking it out on loved ones and feeling extreme anxiety take over. It is often difficult to name it as anger. "Good girls" don't get angry. Loving Christians don't feel animosity toward others. Many of us grew up believing we are "supposed to be" sweet, loving, gentle and kind. We should not raise our voices or speak out our feelings. But we end up sublimating the anger, pushing it down with food, alcohol, guilt and denial. If these issues are not addressed we enter the cyclical war of depression not knowing how to bring it to an end because we have fallen so deep into a pit of misery.

## Anger without Sin

Psychologists tell us that anger is not a bad emotion, nor is it something we need not feel. Even Jesus got angry at the money changers in the temple. He over turned tables to get his point across. Pushing anger down as a way of not dealing with its reality only fuels the negative power that it can wage on our mind, body and spirit. So, if anger isn't necessarily a bad emotion to feel, how can I responsibly exhibit this emotion without doing harm to myself or anyone else? Anger can be a motivator that calls us to action against some injustice in our lives or in others. This type of anger is referred to in the New Testament as *thumos*, it means, "the soul's response to pain, suffering, and injustice." It is what Paul meant when he told believers to be angry but without sin.

## The Effects of Anger on our Bodies and Souls

Researchers have discovered that physiological behaviors prepare our bodies to respond to different types of emotions. Daniel Goleman, author of <u>Emotional Intelligence,</u>" explains, *"when we experience the emotion of anger our blood flows to our hands, which make it easier to grasp a weapon or strike at a foe; our heart rate increases, and a rush of the hormone called adrenaline generates a pulse of energy which is forceful enough to transmit vigorous action. These biological factors are shaped even more by our culture and life experiences."* Psychologists like John Mayer from the University of New Hampshire and Yale's Peter Salovey, a co-formulator on the theory of emotional intelligence, tell us that being aware of an emotion like anger is the first step toward being able to responsibly act on it and change it. Stopping the impulse to hit someone out of anger does not necessarily mean that your feeling of anger has disappeared.

Anger all too often builds on anger much like what putting water on a grease fire does. It ultimately just produces a bigger fire. Daniel Goleman in <u>Emotional Intelligence</u> shares what Psychologist Dolf Zillmann has done on a series of experiments to measure anger and the anatomy of rage. He found that when the body is already in a state of anxiety or edginess, other provoking stimuli can result in an emotional hijacking which can lead to rage. Successive anger-provoking thought or perception becomes a trigger that feeds on the hormonal momentum which can escalate the body's level of physiological arousal. Anger building on anger, heating up and becoming rage without reason which erupts into violence.

We see this scenario played out all too often when a parent becomes so enraged with their child's behavior that they end up lashing out even hitting their child. Or the times when we hold our anger in and chose to avoid conflict at all costs only to find ourselves unleashing its volcanic power. In one big eruption, it covers the person causing our distress plus innocent bystanders who just happen to cross our path at the wrong time.

*Jan* ~ I am constantly reminded in today's world that depression comes from anger turned inward. Due to the havoc that unresolved anger plays on our mind and bodies many of us suffer from different health issues. There is not a person alive who has not at one time or another found themselves building a fence of anger around their hearts. But that only serves to erect a self-made prison that harbors a lifetime of bitterness, resentment, animosity, hostility, aggression, and ill health. Not to mention what destruction it can have on our spiritual lives and our relationship to God and others. The second Greek word for anger in the New Testament is a dangerous one. It is *orge*. It is more than a feeling; it describes what can happen when unanswered anger is allowed to seep deep into the soul, building a wall around the heart. Creating a heart that hardens and festers until rage is born is *orge*, an anger that diminishes the ability or capacity of our heart for love and the forgiveness that love makes possible. Throughout history we hear stories of how people's anger has contributed to the inception of wars, murders, genocide and even suicide. Columbine, kids killing kids, the Holocaust, 9/11, and the Virginia Tech shooting rampage are just a few of the atrocities that come from the inability that humans have in dealing responsibly with the highly charged emotion of anger.

## What Jesus said about Anger

*Jan~* When I think of how Jesus would have handled his anger I am reminded of the scripture passage 1 Peter 2:21, 23 which says, *"For this you have been called, because Christ also suffered for you, leaving you an example that you should follow in his footsteps. He committed no sin, and no deceit was found in his mouth. When he was insulted, he returned no insult; when he suffered, he did not threaten; instead, he handed himself over to the one who judges justly."* The message from that passage is that Jesus gave everything over to God, even his anger. Therefore, for us to give in to our anger is essentially giving up on God. Even the Psalmist in Psalm 30:5 states that *"His anger lasts for a moment, but his favor lasts a lifetime! Weeping may go on all night, but joy comes with the morning."* That is not to say that God tolerates sin and rebellion against him. He is ready to forgive because he is kind and merciful, but only to those who repent and humbly confess their sin and turn to him in faith. In Proverbs 19:11 it says, *"People with good sense restrain their anger; they earn esteem by overlooking wrong."* And in Psalm 4:4 it says, *"Don't sin by letting anger gain control over you. Think about it overnight and remain silent."* It tells us not to instantly react but to take the time to respond after prayerfully gaining God's perspective.

I remember times with my own children when I became so angry at their behavior. In order for me not to become enraged, I would ask them to go to their rooms until I had enough time to pull myself together. I did not want to say something out of my anger that I didn't mean. Nor, did I want to emotionally destroy them by saying something hurtful that would remain locked in their hearts forever. Some parents use the count to ten method before speaking to their children, others need to leave or take a walk to calm down before they confront their children. Everyone needs

117

to find out what works best for them when they are dealing with anger, in order to be able to diffuse their anger and act responsibly and reasonably.

## The emotion of Anger

In the book, <u>Caring Enough to Confront: How to Understand and Express Your deepest Feelings Toward Others</u>, David Augsburger states that *"Anger is a curse, because it is so instantly effective as a way of relieving anxiety. When a person flashes to anger, the anger clouds his recall of what just happened to spark the anger, confuses his awareness of what he is really demanding, and restricts his ability to work toward a new agreement."* This response clouds the reality of dealing and being in touch with how we feel devalued as a person. It is so important for us to become aware of our emotions and the effects that they have on our moods. To be able to identify it, claim it and then be able to work at making a change.

Those of us who engulf ourselves in our emotion of anger and other emotions find it hard to escape them. We no longer are aware of what is really going on, so we become lost in our emotions and feelings. We can become people who have lost all control over our emotional lives and feel highly over-whelmed and unable to escape the mood that anger projects within us. You know who we are talking about, the crabby salesperson, the person that cuts you off in traffic, and drives by giving you an obscene gesture. Or, the angry neighbor who calls you every time your kids steps one foot on his yard. The bitter aunt who blames you and everyone else for her unhappiness, or even the husband who takes out his frustration on the first person that greets him at the door when he comes home from work.

There are those of us who tend to accept whatever we are feeling without trying to change those feelings. People who are susceptible to bad moods which may cause them undue distress, and yet they do nothing to alter those moods. They resign themselves to a life of depression and despair. You know the type, everyone is against me, poor me, nothing is ever going to change so why even try. They remind us of the Disney character, Eeyore, the donkey from Winnie the Pooh, who exhibits traits of depression and moods of feeling sorry for himself, never anticipating life to turn around.

So the question remains how do we defuse our anger? Zillmann believes that we need to take hold of and challenge the very thoughts that are triggering our surges of anger. It is like withholding the fuel that keeps the fire burning. He believes that timing is everything, meaning the earlier in the cycle of anger that we defuse these thoughts by challenging them and understanding them the more effective we will be. Therefore, in order to understand why we put on the mask of anger we need to understand what it is that we are really hiding from. What is this mask of anger really covering up in our lives? Anger can be a response from both physical and emotional pain. Anger can sometimes be easier to deal with then digging deep into our hearts to figure out the true cause of our pain. A lifetime of unexamined hurt can turn us into an unrecognizable person. And unfortunately, once rage is activated, it incapacitates us to use any mitigating information to defuse its destructive tendencies. We no longer can reason or think straight, thus we act out our anger in fits of debilitating and uncontrollable rage. Have you ever experienced such anger that you felt as though you no longer were actually a part of your own body? A Feeling almost as though you were standing outside of yourself, watching a raving lunatic ignite and not being able to do a thing about it? Or maybe you have been a victim to such anger, and you could swear that you no longer recognize or know the person who is discharging their anger at you?

*Jan* ~ I believe that most of us have been on either side of anger's wrath. We are either the one who is angry or we are the victim of someone else's anger. Usually, when I become really angry, the source of my anger is fear. I am acting out of a defensive posture to some injustice done to me or to those whom I care about. This reminds me of the morning I drove my kids to school and was rear ended. After the initial shock of being hit, I checked to see if my kids were ok; one of them was holding the side of their head from having bumped it against the window. I remember storming out of the car like a bear protecting her cubs and yelling and screaming at the woman in the car who had hit us. All I could think about was the health and safety of my children being jeopardized by someone who should have been paying better attention to their driving.

After the police had arrived the officer shared with me information about the woman who had driven into us. She had recently lost her mother and was on depression medication. Although, that was not an excuse for poor driving skills, it helped me to put my anger into perspective. Realizing that my children were going to be alright and that cars can be fixed, I was able to think and act more rationally. I was also able to view the driver of the car as more than just the operator of the vehicle who smashed up my car, but as a human being who was also suffering through trials of her own. It wasn't like she meant to harm my children, or my car, it was just an accident.

## Turning to God when we are Angry

As women, relationships mean everything to us. We are, as psychologists suggest, relational beings. Therefore, our friendships are important to us and when our friends let us down we can feel hurt, rejected, and sometimes even angry.

Women need other women to talk to, pray with, mentor to and share. Many women share from their hearts which make them vulnerable when the person they have shared with lets them down. How many of you have ever felt rejected by someone whom you believed was a close friend? Maybe it was over something that was said about your children, your spouse, or even about you. Maybe, it was just one big misunderstanding, or maybe you and your friend have simply grown in different directions and you no longer see things the same as you once had. How many of us hold grudges as women? Why is it that men seem to be able to get mad at one another one moment and be telling jokes and out playing on the golf course the next? Why do we get our feelings hurt so easily allowing what others think about us to matter so much?

Where does our anger come from when someone we believed was a close friend hurts us or walks out on that friendship? What do we do with those feelings of rejection and anger? Do we try to ignore them, push them down, or do we have to be aware of them, and own them in order to walk through them and into healing? Is feeling angry part of the equation to gaining forgiveness and peace?

The Psalms are filled with people expressing their anger to God about the troubles in their lives. God wants us to come to him with all of our troubles; we need as women to admit to God that we are having feelings of disappointment or anger. God can give us the wisdom and guidance to assess our situation. Sometimes we may be the ones who need to ask for forgiveness and admit that we are wrong. There is often something that we can do that can relieve a bit of the tension to make things better. Although, there are also those times where we must just prayerfully and patiently wait in hopes that the other person will do what is right. The secret is to trust God and acknowledge that which is out of our hands and place the rest into God's hands. For only God's grace can help us to forgive and be at peace with our situation.

## Forgiveness

Choosing to forgive is a tremendous step toward breaking down the fence of anger and pain, and it allows us to enter into a new state of freedom. This takes a lot of courage, to finally let go of the pain from your past and to allow forgiveness to enter in. It's not easy to look past the behavior of those whom have hurt you and to recognize the pain in their lives and their need to be forgiven. It's a conscious choice, one needs to make prayerfully everyday, especially when those feelings of pain, sorrow and anger build up inside of you.

Jan ~ When confronted by my own hurts and anger I try to acknowledge my pain, release it to God, and ask that he help me to forgive others, as he has forgiven me. I am learning to pray for those who have hurt me. I have also learned over my lifetime that whenever you hold something against anyone, you are also holding it in your heart as well. A fenced in heart keeps you from the loving and healing power of God. I choose to give my anger over to God trusting that God will work in my relationships as he wills. And he works all things together for my good and the good of others.

## Creating Healthy Boundaries

Molly ~ For me, I notice it is about boundaries. If others overstep my boundaries or I do not create healthy boundaries for myself, I often feel used, manipulated, under appreciated and not affirmed. But in a way, I have invited that experience and I need to stop and look, to listen to my inner voice that allows me to gain a new perspective on why I gave away my self-worth. Sometimes when I get in touch with that anger,

I am afraid that it is going to consume me that I am so over-whelmed with how strong the feeling is that I will never find balance or peace again.

I remember a particular rough day at work soon after I was married when I was angry at a coworker's comment. I came home physically spent, mentally drained, and when I tried to explain the situation to my husband, I broke out in tears. He said, *"Well then, quit your job!"* I looked at him like he was crazy and blurted out through my sobs, *"I love my job, and I just needed to tell you what happened today that has me so angry!"* It was a profound moment in our marriage. We realized then that we come at things from two totally different pathways. He wanted to fix my problem and I just wanted to vent, to have him listen. Now, he understands that for me, processing means sharing what I am feeling. And then I am able to develop a plan of action. For him, he processes silently and then shares when he has determined a decision he wants to discuss.

### Finding Your Voice

Molly ~ An earlier example of my anger was illustrated to me when I reflected on that experience. In these times God can help us discern our call as we get in touch with our emotional triggers especially anger. When I was 18, I thought my "calling" was Nursing. I remember my first morning on the floor in the hospital, in my crisp student uniform. My first patient was an eighty-five year old woman that I can still see as clear as day some thirty years later. I read the doctor's orders and one of them was "to ambulate her up and down the hall". I went in to her room and asked her if she would like to take a little walk. She said, *"Oh honey, I am so tired. Couldn't we just sit and have a nice chat. Nobody seems to have time for that anymore."* Being the naive student that I was, I pulled a chair up alongside her bed and let her tell me a wonderful story about her love for her deceased husband, how they met, married, and traveled and their devotion to each other for over fifty years until he died the previous year. I realized right then that for her to share those memories was a healing gift and far more important than one walk that day.

When I told the Nursing Instructor what had occurred, she shouted at me, *"I don't care what she wanted; the doctor's orders were to ambulate her down the hall."* I remember walking back to the dorm that September morning in 1972 and being so angry! "What about her voice, what about what she wanted? What about my voice? Is playing by the rules always more important?" After being in health care for twenty-five years my focus evolved to patient education and patient advocacy. Needless to say, my frustrations continued to grow with the realization that even though many were physically ill, some with the prognosis of good recovery, others not, still many had lost their hope. And many failed to feel God's presence in their suffering. I began to become more concerned with their spiritual disease. I would try to avail myself so that they could give "voice" to those inner conflicts that they could not share with family or friends. I became enamored with their stories and wanted to walk with them on their spiritual journeys. It made me reflect on the beginning of my career that autumn day of my freshman year at college. I think in this moment God was calling me into the ministry of Spiritual Direction. It just took me a while to listen and act on God's wisdom.

**Taking it to Heart**

God tells us to not let the sun go down on our anger. Insightful wisdom from God advises all of us to not hold onto our ill feelings, but to release them; to plant them at the tree on Calvary. It is God who can help us get rid of our anger. *"The Lord heals all diseases"* (PS. 103:2-3 NIV). The affliction of anger is no different from someone who has unjustified fears or phobias. Any emotion that keeps us from being the person God wants us to be is unhealthy. An angry heart needs healing and only God can heal it. The question becomes do we want him to? The same question that Jesus asks of the invalid in scripture God asks of us, do we want to be well?

**Scripture Reflections**

### Psalm 18:12 NIV
*Who can discern his errors? Forgive my hidden faults*

### Matthew 5:7 NIV
*Blessed are the merciful, for they shall obtain mercy.*

### I Corinthians 13:5 CEV
*Love isn't selfish or quick tempered. It doesn't keep a record of wrongs that others do.*

### Mark 11:25
*Whenever you stand praying, forgive if you have anything against anyone; so that your Father in heaven may also forgive you your trespasses.*

### Micah 7:18
*Who is a God like you, pardoning iniquity*
*And passing over the transgression*
*Of the remnant of your possession?*
*He does not retain his anger forever,*
*Because he delights in showing clemency.*

What do **Proverbs 19:11** and **Psalm 4:4** tell us about our anger and what we should do with it? How do you deal with your anger? What might you do differently after reading these passages?

_____

_____

_____

**Workbook Questions**

1. Is anger a sin?

2. Is it okay to be angry?

3. How does anger manifest itself in your life?

4. How do you face anger, confront it, and then find a solution?

5. What are the underlying issues or roots of anger in your life?

6. What are some healthy ways in which you can deal with your anger?

7. What did Jesus do when He was angry?

8. What does Scripture suggest that we do when we feel angry?

9. Are you afraid to confront your anger and why or why not?

10. Have we been conditioned as women that it is not acceptable to get angry?

11. Are you afraid that your anger will overwhelm you?

12. How might we lose our voice when we are angry?

13. What do you do when you know that others are angry at you?

14. Have you ever felt angry at God? Explain?

15. What are some healthy ways to deal with anger?

16. What are some of the physiological responses that you notice whenever you encounter anger?

17. Can you get to a place where you can actually feel at peace about dealing appropriately with your anger and not feel guilty?

18. Can forgiveness resolve your anger?

19. Can God help you to resolve your anger and find peace? Explain how God does this for you?

**Prayer Affirmations:**

1. God forgive me for the sinful anger in my life. Give me the courage and the strength to face my emotional wounds. Help me to forgive those who have hurt me and free me from this fortress of anger that I have built around my heart. I ask this in your name.
   Amen

2. God knowing and understanding the connection between the emotion of anger and illnesses please help me to examine the pain at the heart of my anger in order to destroy its debilitating and harmful effects on my health and on those around me. I ask this in your name.
   Amen

**Journaling from the Heart**

How can you experience anger in your life that is healthy and does not cause you to sin? For example: anger that motivates you to correct an injustice and stand against oppression.

_____

_____

_____

_____

_____

_____

_____

_____

_____

_____

_____

_____

_____

_____

_____

_____

_____

_____

_____

_____

_____

_____

_____

_____

# 7

# FENCES OF FEAR

## Freedom to Trust the Holy Spirit in Your Heart

*The fear of man brings a snare, but whoever puts his trust in the Lord shall be safe Proverbs 29:25 (MKJV)*

How many of you act or choose not to act out of some sense of fear? Fear tends to run your life or others around you? Some fears are debilitating, they rob you of your very freedom to live a full and graced life. Fear is everywhere, in the person who won't ever leave their home, drive a car, fly on a plane, or commit to a relationship. Fear can hold us back from the very desires of our hearts and Gods. How many people might we have helped or even saved if only we would have allowed ourselves? By making the decision to push past our fears by reaching out instead of letting them hold us back.

Our fear often stem from our prejudice, ignorance, or doubts about the unknown. How much fear has been passed down from one generation to another, from one culture or society to another? Is it ever good to be afraid? Is fear an emotion that comes from God? Is it something that we conjure up in our conscious and subconscious minds, keeping us from doing God's work? There are so many examples of those who work against fear. Like the stranger who runs back into a burning building to save someone that he or she doesn't even know. Or even the missionary who gives their life to bring the Good News to those without access to the message. Or the soldier who dies so that others might be free. Even the child who stands up to the bully on the playground? What is it that makes one person resist the strangling hold of fear on their lives and another who fall prey to its suffocating and defying grip?

## Love Casts Out All Fear

What does God say about fear? How can I overcome it when it engulfs me in its clutches and find the strength to go on? In Psalm 46:1-2 it says, "God *is our refuge and strength, always ready to help in times of trouble. So we will not fear, even if earthquakes come and the mountains crumble into the sea."* In John 14:27 it says, *"I am leaving you with a gift—peace of mind and heart. And the peace I give isn't like the peace the world gives. So don't be troubled or afraid."* And in 2 Timothy 1:7 it says, *"God had not given us a spirit of fear and timidity, but of power, love and self-discipline."* We've heard as Christians that fear does not come from the Lord. When fear erects its fence around our hearts we must choose to call upon God's Spirit to give us the grace and power to face our foes. We must let his love overcome any evil with good. We also need discipline to persevere through our darkest trials; turning our fear into trust, faith and hope in the God that created and loves us. God is our light and salvation, God is our refuge and place of safety as the Psalmist wrote in Psalms 27 and 91.

*Jan* ~ I don't think when I was growing up that parents were as open with their children as we are today. My husband and I talked and included our children in just about everything that was going on in our family and in the world. Ken and I always tried to respect their opinions and we would have family meetings to discuss whatever issues might needed to be addressed at that time in our lives. We prayed, cried and laughed together, sharing some of our deepest concerns with one another. We also learned the importance of keeping our children safe by sharing information that we would hope help to protect them in most situations.

My parents' generation often times kept things to themselves for fear that sharing information might scare their children or cause unnecessary worry. In some ways, it allowed us to be children longer. Times were also much simpler back when I was young. We didn't hear about all of the atrocities that we deal with today; like children being abducted from their very own bedrooms, backyards, and shopping centers. Or the looming predators hidden in our children's chat rooms on the internet.

With the world being a very different place from the one that I grew up in, I insisted on driving my children anywhere they wanted to go. "Don't ever talk to strangers," was a motto we drilled into our girls and it was not a message that neither Ken nor I can remember our parents addressing. Our girls are now in college and I still catch myself telling them to be careful, alert, and observant of those around them. I am constantly sending them messages and emails, reminding them to have their key out and ready before they go out to the car, and then to look in the back seat before getting in. They have heard plenty of lectures to never go into a public restroom alone, or take walks out late at night by themselves. Was it out of my fear that I felt I needed to protect my children or am I sadly living in a time where it is necessary to make them aware of the evil that exists in our world in order to keep them safe? Maybe, it is not so much fear as it is to help them to set healthy boundaries, to learn to use common sense in all things by praying, listening, and discerning before acting or reacting.

## Trusting God's Messenger

*Jan* ~ I will share a story that happened when I was twelve, over thirty nine years ago during a snow storm. Back then it was nothing for children to walk a mile or two to their school, friend's house, or the local candy store, without the accompaniment of a parent or an older guardian. Most families only had one car. Dad was generally the one using the car for work during the day. It was a more trusting time when people left their houses and cars unlocked, and windows open. Children were often left unattended playing in the front yard, or down around the block with friends until dark. I was one of those young girls that had a tremendous amount of energy, an extreme extrovert that loved people. I was so outgoing that my parents often said that I could even have a conversation with a tree if no one else was available to converse with.

As I read Psalm 91:1-7, 11 I found it to resonate with my story, a story that I believe I would not have been able to share with you today if my parents had not taught me how to pray. Remember to have faith, and listen to the voice of God. The Psalmist states,

> *"Those who live in the shelter of the Most High will find rest in the shadow of the Almighty. This I declare of the lord: He alone is my refuge, my place of safety; he is my God, and I am trusting him. For he will rescue you from every trap and protect you from the fatal plague. He will shield you with his wings. He will shelter you with his feathers. His faithful promises are your armor and protection. Do not be afraid of the terrors of the night, nor fear the dangers of*

*the day, nor dread the plague that stalks in dark-
ness, nor the disaster that strikes at midday. Though
a thousand fall at your side, though ten thousand are
dying around you, these evils will not touch you... He
orders his angels to protect you wherever you go.*"

Being the energetic, friendly, and outgoing twelve year
that I was, I had many friends that were spaced throughout
our small suburban city, just outside of Detroit. One friend
invited me over that cold, snowy winter day to go ice skating
on the pond behind her house. Unfortunately, she was the
friend who lived the farthest away from my home and my
parents could not offer me a ride. The wintry weather was
showing no signs of letting up, so after receiving my mother's permission to let me walk, I bundled up. I grabbed my
ice skates, coat, scarf, hat and mittens and ran out the door
excited to make an adventure of it.

After trudging through the deep snow for over a mile,
I decided to devise a plan that could get me to my friend's
house a bit quicker, avoiding any cars on the main roads. I
remembered from playing at my friend's house last summer
that we had taken a short cut down a dead end street. When
we got to the end we went through some woods which
brought us right into my friend's subdivision.

The snow was still coming down at a steady pace as I
turned onto the dead end street. I decided to walk down the
middle of the road to avoid the high drifts on either side. I
had assured myself that I probably would not be encountering
much traffic due to the snowy weather conditions and slip-
pery roads. I can still remember what the snowflakes looked
like as they fell down from the sky that afternoon, reminding
me of one of those snow globes that you shake upside down.
I also observed how different the houses looked than I had
remembered. Many of them were boarded up now with no
signs of life or activity. It puzzled me that there were no

kids anywhere playing in the yards, building snowmen, or engaging in a snowball fight.

At first, I was amazed at how quickly I became aware of my surroundings, and of how I felt as the beautiful snowflakes kissed my face. In that exact moment of elation, I was suddenly hit with this odd sense of doom and it sent shivers up my spine. It was then that I heard an audible voice inside me; it called to me by name and told me not to be afraid. Immediately, I looked around me to see who might be calling out to me but to my astonishment no one was there. There were no signs of any activity coming from any of the houses that I passed; just an odd sense of peace and stillness that seemed to comfort me in that moment. Next, I remember thinking and saying to myself, "*what a silly and active imagination I have, I must be talking to myself.*" It was right then that the voice again called me by my name, "*Janis do not to be afraid,*" and then encouraged me to be still and listen for further instructions.

Next, I was warned that a car would soon be turning down the dead end street and that the man inside of the car wanted to hurt me. I was advised that I needed to stay calm but that I should start running toward the woods at the end of the street. The voice informed me that there would be a house near the edge of the woods that appeared livable where I would need to seek refuge from the ominous man in the soon to be approaching vehicle. Confused and frightened, I started to run as fast as I could, looking back over my shoulder to see if anyone was coming. When I was only a few houses away from the streets dead end, the voice told me that the driver and the car were just turning onto my street. As I glanced over my shoulder sure enough a car far in the distance had turned. Before the car reached me, the voice assured me once again to not be afraid. It told me that when I got to the last house I was to run towards it and yell, "*NO,*

*I LIVE HERE*" as loud as I could. I was to make my way toward the side door where I could hide and be safe. I was told to remain there until the voice advised me that it was safe to come out.

Amazingly, the car stopped right in front of the very house I was told I would find protection. The man swung open the passenger side of his vehicle, and yelled for me to get in. After I yelled back and ran to the side of the house for refuge, I cautiously peeked out and watched him do dough-nuts in the snow as he tried to regain traction and leave. Once he had gotten back onto the main road the voice informed me that it was safe to come out and make my way through the woods to my friend's house.

Needless to say that experience changed my life. Not only had I experienced something that was extraordinary and miraculous it taught me the importance of both listening for God's voice and trusting in God's protection. As the Psalmist wrote, *"He alone is my refuge, my place of safety; he is my God, and I am trusting him. His faithful promises are my armor and protection. I will not be afraid of the terrors of the night, nor fear the dangers of the day, nor dread the plague that stalks in darkness, nor the disaster that strikes at midday. He orders his angels to protect me wherever I go"* (Psalm 91).

## God's Revelation

Fear is one of those fences that we so often need to work through in order for it not to paralyze us and keep us from being the person that God has created us to be. We are only able to accomplish that by placing our trust in God. In Jeremiah 17:7-8 it states *"Blessed are those who trust in the Lord, whose trust is the lord, they shall be like a tree planted by water, sending out its roots by the stream. It shall not fear when heat comes, and its leaves shall stay green; in the year of drought it is not anxious and it does not cease to bear fruit."* Fear builds a fence in our lives when we fail to plug into the very source that made us. Just as the roots of a tree need to be nourished by the water given by the stream, we need to be nourished through our relationship with God. Our lives will only produce fruit and take on meaning when we are connected to our creator. Trust in and our Love for God casts out all fear.

The question then that we really need to ask ourselves is, who do we allow to control our lives, our fears or our God? When we allow our fears to erect a fence around our hearts, we block out the very presence of our God. We need to dismantle that which we have constructed by trusting in God's sovereign will. I can do this by imitating what Jesus taught me and continues to teach me each time I get in touch with God's Word in the Bible. If I allow what others say about me or what false teachers tell me about who I am and who I am not, I am looking for my answers outside of God's revelation. Therefore, I am putting more importance and trust into others opinions then on God.

Don't we all at sometime in our lives look for the quick fix to our problems? Our fears of not being liked, of being too fat, or too skinny, or not pretty enough, or rich enough, funny or smart enough all leads us to engage in participating in all of the world's latest schemes, remedies, diets, fads, and personality tools that eventually bring us back full circle with more fears and senseless searching. When all along all we had to do was to look deep within ourselves. To find and use the gifts that God has given each of us, and to see with the eyes of faith that it is Christ who supplies all of our answers through His gift of the Holy Spirit.

It's about projecting a world view that says I want to be more like Christ; I want to follow His teachings, His example, and His ways. Knowing that I was made in God's own image and likeness, I want to imitate His behavior, to ask the Holy

Spirit that lives within me what would Jesus have done about the problems and fears that I am now facing. What do the Scriptures say about my situation? Can any of my answers be found in those Saints that lived before me? Has God not already revealed so many of the answers to my questions and fears through the countless stories discussed in the Bible? Learning to apply what it is that God reveals through His Word to my own life experiences is key to purge the fears that keep me from experiencing a closer relationship with God and with others.

Whenever our fears keep us from living our lives in and through Christ, we need to step back and revaluate the decisions and choices that we are making based on those fears. It's a matter of asking ourselves what Jesus would do in my situation. How can I apply what I learn from Scripture to the situation that I am currently in? What does God's Word say about what I am feeling, saying, doing, or not doing? Prayer and discernment are key factors to making any choices or decisions in our lives. God is our lifeline, the one in which all of us need to call upon first before acting on our fears. There is no better physician, counselor, psychologist, therapist, or teacher that we can bring our fears to then our very own Creator Almighty God. Jesus Christ is our one and only Savior, so next time your fears begin to take over your life, choose to give them over to God, lay them down at the foot of the cross and leave them there. Only God can set you free and give your heart the peace that you have so longed for.

## Fear Not

*Molly* ~ In discussing my own sense of fear, I am reminded on how often Jesus challenges me in the Scriptures to "fear not" and how difficult I find this to do. I wonder if it would be helpful to consider what it would have been like to be one of Jesus' actual followers. Would it make me less fearful about situations in which I am afraid of failing or disappointing others?

My first impression is of walking beside a gentle man who is socially conscious and just. He rooted for the underdog, wanting all to hear his Voice so that all may share in a personal relationship with God, our Father. If I close my eyes and imagine that I am there, perhaps on that road to Emmaus, I see that I am tired and dusty. The sun is directly overhead and all I can think about is a cool drink for my parched lips. I'm lost in thought, aware that someone is walking along beside me. Surprisingly, I do not feel threatened by his close proximity, instead I look and notice how peaceful and calm he appears, how unfettered by the heat and dry surroundings. He almost seems refreshed! He speaks in such a quiet tone, that I lean inward to hear what he is saying. He is talking about how foolish we are and slow of heart to not believe all that the prophets have spoken. How does he understand what I have been struggling with? If God has raised Jesus, then anything can happen. God can do anything! My fear and despair have been cautiously transforming into confidence and joy. I am starting to think anything is possible. I feel free.

But how can I truly hear his Voice unless I understand the cultural context from which Jesus immigrated? Was my experience of what I imagined it was like walking with Jesus similar to those who were there to hear his words? How did his one true Voice profoundly challenge them in their own spiritual journey?

Although the New Testament is influenced by both Israel and Greece, Jesus is a Jew and the lifestyle of the Jews is markedly different from the agrarian people of Greece who settled in one place. For the Jewish people, each stop along the way represents both a fulfillment of the day's accomplishments and a looking forward to the next day's successes. They live by hope in the promises of God and trust in his covenant with them. Their concept of "Kingdom of God" referred to God's continual activity of creating the world on behalf of His people. They were on the lookout for God to reverse the present situation through some cosmic future triumph that would establish Israel and defeat all her enemies. For Jesus' notion of Kingdom of God differed from the Israelite's concept. For Jesus, the reign of God is not a place or a community ruled by God. It is saying yes to God's touch, and in so doing, allowing God to become active and present.

Once Jesus came along, the world of the Pharisees was upended. Jesus spoke in parables, and unlike future generations who would read these passages as example stories, or allegories, for Jesus' contemporaries, his message reversed their expectations and turned fundamental beliefs and assumptions upside down. He challenges their irreversible truth. In his parables, the listeners expected the priest and the Levite to give aid to the wounded Jew in the Good Samaritan story (Luke 15:11-32). They thought for sure that the parents would reward the faithful child and punish the wayward one in the Prodigal Son (Luke 14:15-24). And everyone knew you throw a dinner party for friends, not strangers as happened in the Banquet setting (Luke 14:15-24). What actually happens in the parable is the reverse of what the listener expects. The parables, as did Jesus, seemed to evoke uncertainty and ambiguity. Jesus exposed false idols and made present God's reign. People were left to see and hear, to be converted and healed or to shut out the truth. The disciples were desolate when they realized Jesus had ultimately died. Even Jesus experienced the humanness of feeling utterly abandoned on the cross. But only through death can come resurrection. Once some of Jesus' followers realized he had truly risen from the grave, their hope was restored. They experienced new life. The darkness they had felt was now filled with exhilaration and light.

The faith experience that Jesus provokes among some people, especially his disciples, is one that resonates with my own spiritual journey. I look first at the Pharisees. For them ethics precedes and determines salvation. One obeys the Law so that God will save. The Torah and its laws created a sense of personal and social security... and in this picture I see a snapshot of my own life before I too was "parabled" by Jesus.

## Listening to my Authentic God Voice

Molly ~ I was the "good" Catholic girl, the oldest always taking care of my siblings, following all the rules, an "A" student, class Valedictorian going to Nursing school at the University of Michigan. God was "out there": Someone I prayed to before test time or worshiped and revered in Mass and Eucharist. He was distant, omnipotent, and Someone Else to please. Like one of my teachers, I just wanted an "A" in His classroom, and needed to know what was expected of me so I could invoke his favor and acceptance.

On a warm August night, the year of my 26th birthday, my sister and her fiancé were having a party and asked me to stop over. I remember being immediately attracted to a tall, blonde-haired man who stood filling ice trays at the kitchen sink. Kath, my sister introduced us. His name was Paul and it felt like we had conversed for minutes, when in actuality hours were slipping by. The ease I felt with him was ironic considering his circumstances. He had recently ended a long term relationship, and obviously was not ready for jumping into another serious commitment. But it was one of those nights I knew I would never forget. I knew that without a doubt God had brought him into my life for a reason, but I was being stretched in new directions. Everything I had experienced in previous relationships felt challenged and suspect. I often sensed a fear of commitment and uneasiness in my past dating rituals and at times felt like just wanting to run away.

Paul did not call after that night for four months, and I learned in that time that I had to surrender, relinquish control and trust God that if it was meant to be something would change. On a rainy December day, Paul was heading out for lunch, and stopped at a busy intersection. There, lying on the side of the road was a black man. Cars were passing by when Paul saw him, stopped, and pulled his rain-soaked body into the car. He wore a medical bracelet that revealed that he was an epileptic and that his doctor was John Anderson at the Family Health Center at St. Mary's Hospital. Paul brought him to the hospital and got him the help he needed. While waiting, he recalled that I had mentioned I worked there and so after the patient was stabilized, he asked the receptionist if I was on duty. I got a page to go to the coffee room and when I saw Paul standing there I felt as if I had come home, and from that moment on we started dating.

Soon my parents and friends realized how serious the relationship had become, and I felt alive for the first time in my life. I could totally be myself and Paul loved me unconditionally. How could this be wrong when I felt such peace?

When Paul asked me to marry him, I answered yes with every fiber of my being. It was as though the little girl that had withered under all the stress and strain of trying to be what everyone expected began to blossom into a beautiful child of God. That still small voice inside found resonance in my quiet whisper and shouted in a God-voice I had never known.

Just as I had imagined, the impressions I felt when Jesus was walking beside me, these were the same comfortable feelings being with Paul evoked. Jesus' acquaintances knew him as the carpenter's son from Nazareth. Just as he challenges me today when I am confronted with social justice issues in society, I have to stop and ask myself how come I can not look the other way. Just as Paul gave aid to the poor soul on the street, I can not be silent anymore and fail to respond to those voices that stir within me. I have to listen to that Voice again and speak my truth. When I am willing to admit I do not have it all figured out, that I am totally and utterly confused, only then can the reign of God takeover.

I am not in control. I grew up in a country where self-sufficiency was supported on all sides. I received good grades to get into college. I chose a career to be successful, to improve my standing in the community, help others, and "feel fulfilled." It is amazing to me that our own acquaintances ask what we do, instead of what we think or feel. The acquisitions, careers, promotions, and families do not make us happy. Conversion came when I heard with my heart, and my eyes and ears were open. But once that happened, my life was never the same. It demanded that I change, and that I take risks.

Once I realized how much I loved Paul and how right it felt in my heart, I knew my comfortable and complacent life was gone and the unknown was to be my truth. This upending is what Jesus is all about.

Just as the Pharisees understanding of salvation looked toward the future, if I think only about tomorrow, I will miss that God is reigning here and now. The Pharisees thought by obeying the laws of the Torah the kingdom of God would be theirs. I believed that if I followed all the rules and the "shoulds," I would be happy. In both instances we are trying to control God. We are telling God how to respond. Much of what Jesus did seem to contradict the Jewish law. Jesus lived his life in fidelity to God rather than obedience to the Law. For Jesus, the proclamation of the kingdom of God is the focus of all of his teachings. He saw it as a personal experience, one that transforms human relationships, and not as a future event. Jesus helps us to understand that God's kingdom is God's alone, and once I surrender "my stuff" and accept that I am not in charge; there is a huge sense of freedom that results from that leap of faith. My willingness to trust the God-voice within me helped me to realize what a life-changing event that could be. When I stripped away all the outside noise and listened to that dormant little whisper, it transformed my journey. I understood that to reach out for new life, a part of me had to die forever. And the freedom and joy has infused in me a passion to affirm and validate the God-voice in others as a Spiritual Director. My ministry is truly a fruit of the Spirit. Being "parabled" brought me to faith; a faith that celebrates my total, unequivocal trust in the Creator. Not a religion of rules and obligations, but spirituality with a God who loves me just as I am, and whom I embrace as my beloved "Abba".

**Workbook Questions**

1. What do you fear the most? Why as a woman of faith should you not be afraid?

2. What does God say about fear in Scripture, and how can you apply that to your own life?

3. What Christian tools could you use to overcome your fears?

4. Many scripture passages say that we need to fear God, does that mean that we should be afraid of God? What do you think to fear God means?

5. How can your fears keep you from growing closer to God? How do your fears stop you from having other healthy relationships? Explain?

6. How might you help someone else overcome their fears?

7. What is the difference between peace and fear? And how can trusting in God help you to overcome fear?

**Taking it to Heart**

May we not be so caught up in agonizing about our past, worrying about our todays, and fearing our tomorrows? May we learn to live each day as a gift as it was graciously given to us by God. May we trust God with our whole hearts and be anxious for nothing. Help us to remember that there is no fear in love, and that love casts out all fear. Therefore, we must call on God, who is the very essence of love to drive out all fears that keep our hearts imprisoned and our voices silenced.

**Scripture Reflections**

**Set aside time each week to reflect on this Psalm in order to reveal in your heart the truth that God is shepherding you and therefore you have nothing to fear.**

**Psalm 23** *"The Lord is my shepherd; I shall not want He maketh me to lie down in green pastures: he leadeth me beside the still waters He restoreth my soul: he leadeth me in the paths of righteousness for his name's sake. Yea, though I walk through the valley of the shadow of death, I will fear no evil: for thou art with me; thy rod and thy staff they comfort me. Thou preparest a table before me in the presence of mine enemies; thou Anointest my head with oil; my cup runneth over. Surely goodness and mercy shall follow me all the days of my life; and I will dwell in the house of the Lord forever. (KJV)*

**After reading each of these scripture passages rewrite them using your own words.**

**Jeremiah 17: 7-8** *Blessed are those who trust in the Lord, whose trust is the lord, they shall be like a tree planted by water, sending out its roots by the stream. It shall not fear when heat comes, and its leaves shall stay green; in the year of drought it is not anxious and it does not cease to bear fruit.*

---
---

**Psalm 91:7** *"Those who live in the shelter of the Most High will find rest in the shadow of the Almighty. This I declare of the lord: He alone is my refuge, my place of safety; he is my God, and I am trusting him. For he will rescue you from every trap and protect you from the fatal plague. He will shield you with his wings. He will shelter you with his feathers. His faithful promises are your armor and protection. Do not be afraid of the terrors of the night, nor fear the dangers of the day, nor dread the plague that stalks in darkness, nor the disaster that strikes at midday. Though a thousand fall at your side, though ten thousand are dying around you, these evils will not touch you... He orders his angels to protect you wherever you go."*

---
---
---
---

**Psalm 46:1-2** *God is our refuge and strength, a very present help in trouble. Therefore will not we fear through the earth be removed, and though the mountains be carried into the midst of the sea. (NIV)*

---
---
---

**John 14: 27** *Peace I leave with you, my peace I give unto you: not as the world giveth, I give unto you. Let not your heart be troubled, neither let it be afraid. (NIV)*

_____

_____

_____

_____

_____

**1 John 4:18** *There is no fear in love, but perfect love casts out fear, because fear has torment. He who fears has not been perfected in love. (MKJV)*

_____

_____

_____

_____

_____

**2 Timothy 1:7** *God did not give us a spirit of timidity, but the Spirit of power and love and self-control. (New Jerusalem Bible)*

_____

_____

_____

_____

_____

**Prayer Affirmations:**

1. God, please help me to battle the spirit of fear in my life. Free me from fears unhealthy and debilitating that take hold of my life. Show me the power of your love to cast out all fears in my life and to put all my trust in you so that I might have the faith to fight the battles that you call me to and be pleasing in your sight. *Amen*

**Below draw two pictures, one that resembles fear and one that reveals peace and contentment.**

## Journaling from the Heart

Share a time when you felt alone and afraid, what did that feel like? Now share how it feels to know that God is your Shepherd that God will never abandon or forsake you. That God is your strength and your refuge. God loves you so much that he sacrificed his only Son, Jesus Christ to death on a cross, so that you could live. Knowing these truths and knowing that God is love and that love casts out all fear, how does that now change the way you look at fear, and what in your relationship with God helped to change it?

_____

_____

_____

_____

_____

_____

_____

_____

_____

_____

_____

_____

_____

_____

_____

_____

_____

_____

# Epilogue

*Wisdom comes from listening to what the heart already knows. Unknown author*

The purpose of our book was to open a gate for you. And to help you discover your God voice through the indwelling presence of the Holy Spirit that lives deep within your hearts. *"That the God of our Lord Jesus Christ, the Father of glory, may give you a spirit of wisdom and revelation resulting in knowledge of him and that the eyes of (your) hearts be enlightened, that you may know what is the hope that belongs to his call, and what is the surpassing greatness of his power for us who believe, in accord with the exercise of his great might, worked out in and through Christ"* (Eph.17-19). *(NAB)*

## Walk In the Spirit

We have shared with you some of our own life stories and experiences. Through spiritual insights we learned how to apply God's word in scripture to those experiences. We each have our own unique story to tell; and as women, many of our stories share commonalities with each other. We are therefore not so alone in our spiritual journey and our search for truth, love, peace, mercy, and forgiveness. Our shared stories can become sacred truths and profound lessons of wisdom to be shared with others.

So how do we avoid the very fences and obstacles that we build around our hearts that keeps us from walking in the Spirit? The answer is found in the Holy Spirit that lives within all of us as our God Voice; the voice that directs and guides one to live like Christ. When we listen to that voice alone and act accordingly we will experience the fruit of our labor. All of the fences that we erect in our lives come from living in the flesh and not in the Spirit. Our hearts become prisoners of the flesh, controlled by our impulses, addictions, and compulsions; all those self-made fences that keeps us from growing spiritually, from loving fully, and from fulfilling God's purposes for our lives. When we listen to our God voice we are connected to the Holy Spirit that dwells within us. And when we put the Spirit's guidance into action all of our false fortresses begin to fall away and what remains standing is our authentic and true self. The person who was created in God's own image and likeness, the person who walks in the ways and teachings of Christ. Unless we get in touch with our God voice within we go unprotected from the evils that pursue us in this world.

What better place to discover and use your God voice than in relationships with other Christian women. All of us women need a safe place to go where we can share our authentic selves, our vulnerabilities, our faith and our life stories. Involvement in a Women's ministry gives us the opportunities to share those life fences that we erect around our hearts and helps us to begin to dismantle those self-made fences and walls, through prayer, sharing, compassion, empathy and forgiveness. We learn that we are not alone in our journeys; that we can find other women of faith that can mentor, encourage and empower us to be all that

God created us to be. One of the songs that Molly and I like is called "The Sheltering Tree." When we are struggling, when we feel detached from God, we often turn to music for comfort. This song released by New Song reminds us of what Praying Hearts purpose here is. This song was written by Eddie Carswell and Leonard Ahlstrom. The song talks about how, "we all need friends, like sheltering trees, who will get down on their knees and lift us up before the King of Kings." We hope you will have the opportunity to hear it and that it touches you the way it did us.

We as women do not have to continue to feel isolated and alone in our faith and in our trials. We can opt to put gates in the fences that surround our hearts and allow others and God to enter in. We can become "sheltering trees" and begin to live in true community with God and with one another. Our hearts finally free to glorify God and to fulfill God's purpose.

## Step through the Gate

God continues to invite us into relationship with him and through the sacrifice of God's only begotten Son we have been given the gift to enter in. In the scripture passage John 10:6-7, Jesus tells this simple story, "*I am the Gate for the sheep. I am the Gate. Anyone who goes through me will be cared for- will freely go in and out, and find pasture. A thief is only there to steal and kill and destroy. I came so they can have real and eternal life, more and better life than they ever dreamed of*". (*The Message*) In John 10:3 "*The watchman opens the gate for him, and the sheep listen to his voice. He calls his own sheep by name and leads them out.*" John 10:9 says, "*I am the gate; whoever enters through me will be saved. (NIV)* And in Luke13:24 it says, "*Strive to enter in at the strait gate: for many, I say unto you, will seek to enter in, and shall not be able.*" (*KJV*)

155

Our prayer for you is that you discover that "still small voice," within you that is God and that you are awakened to God's grace working in your life and in others. May you never forget to put up the gate, and unlock your heart to invite Christ in. Follow his voice of love, and allow God to tear down the fences you have built around your hearts that keep you from growing in your faith and love for God and others. Find God's indwelling voice within your heart and begin to experience the freedom that only God and his grace can give, a heart free to love and be loved.

# Notes

1. *Clowning in Rome*, p.52. Henri Nouwen
2. *Heart of the Enlightened*, Anthony de Mello (London: Fount, 1997) p.99.
3  *The Hunger of the Heart:* Ron DelBene,
4. *"In the Garden,"* Christian Hymn written by C. Austin Miles (1868-1941)
5. By Way of the Heart, by Wilkie Au
6. *A Call to Spiritual Growth, Rilke's Book of Hours* by Rainier Maria Rilke
7. *Mending Walls* a poem by Robert Frost
8. *"The Cross of Peace"*, Sir Phillips Gibbs
9. *The Heart's Journey through the Seasons: the Circle of Life* p254: Macrina Wiederkehr
10. *The Awakening Call* a quote from James Finley
11. *Reason Informed By Faith* by Richard M. Gula, quotes James Gustafason S.S. pg51
12. November 1999 document issued by the American bishops, entitled *Our Hearts Were Burning Within Us*
13. *"Julian of Norwich Showings"* (L43, 255).
14. *"The Call"* by Oriah Mountain Dreamer
15. *"The Master's Touch"* by Myra Brooks Welch
16. *Emotional Intelligence*, Daniel Goleman pp6, 7.

17. *Emotional Intelligence*, Daniel Goleman pp 60-62 referring to (Dolf Zillmann)
18. Caring *Enough to Confront: How to Understand and Express Your deepest Feelings Toward Others,* David Augsburger
19. *"Sheltering Tree"*, by song artists Newsong

# Endorsements

"*Unlocking Our Fenced In Hearts*" is a great resource for those who would like to get to the heart of the matter – that is, to discover or rediscover God's unconditional love for them. The exercises in the book are helpful ways to open the hearts to receive God's love and to respond to it by living lives of love in our world today.

Fr. Loc Trinh, Pastor of St. John Vianney Catholic Church Wyoming, Michigan

Having read "*Unlocking Our Fenced In Hearts*," I highly commend Jan and Molly for their efforts in putting it together. Their honesty and personal recollections will be of great help to others in their search for a deeper relationship with our Lord and Savior, Jesus Christ. For each of us, our past becomes part of the dance with our present, which leads to a bountiful future.

The Reverend Grace Coleman Anthony, Rector of St. Paul's Anglican Church Point Edward, Ontario, Canada.

# Authors Biographies

J anis Wasco's great love for the Scriptures led her to first participate in and now lead an array of Bible studies, teaching and Ministerial workshops and seminars. Jan's life has been a process of prayerful, personal discernment to find her God voice which became the catalyst for her returning to college to study Theology, gaining a second Bachelor's and ultimately a Masters in Pastoral Studies. Jan's personal ministry experience is as a loving wife and mother. Some of her faith community work includes serving as a Stephen Minister, Bible study Director, Religious Education high school teacher, facilitator of "Parenting with Love & Logic", and Youth camp Staff Counselor and Coordinator. She has also served in facilitating "Rainbows" for children of divorce, "Moms In Touch", "RCIA" (Right of Christian Initiation for Adults), Right to Life, and as a Captain for women's silent prayer retreats.

Molly Keating is passionate about the voice that comes out of the stillness of each heart. As a Spiritual Director since 1998 she has had the privilege of walking with others on this incredible transformative journey in which one deepens their relationship with God and listens to the guidance, comfort and consolation of the Holy Spirit. She is active in Contemplative Outreach leading workshops, facilitating centering prayer groups and presenting the gift of practicing a method of prayer that awakens one to the indwelling presence of Christ in their everyday experience. She resides with her husband Paul in Grand Rapids, MI.

Printed in the United States
203267BV00002B/184-261/P